Global Solutions

Global Solutions

✦

An internet community takes on globalisation

The consensus of seventy forum participants from North America, Europe, Asia, Africa, and Australia

edited by

Adriaan Boiten
Richard Alden Stimson

iUniverse, Inc.

New York Lincoln Shanghai

Global Solutions
An internet community takes on globalisation

iUniverse, Inc.

For information address:
iUniverse, Inc.
2021 Pine Lake Road, Suite 100
Lincoln, NE 68512
www.iuniverse.com

Published electronically March 2003 by Westchester Press

To contact the editors:
Adriaan Boiten, aboiten@xs4all.nl
Richard Stimson, stimso1@juno.com

ISBN: 0-595-28067-6

Printed in the United States of America

Contents

Introduction—How This Book Was Written Democratically

The origin of this book is quite unusual. Most books have one author, sometimes two, but this book is the product of collaboration by a large number of people in many countries participating in an Internet forum.

Defying the adage that the only piece of good writing by committee was the King James Version of the Bible, the members of this forum set out to create a guide for reform of government at all levels from global down to local communities. They aimed especially to counter global control by financial interests at the expense of democratic self-rule.

It all started in August 2000 when the Internet forum "FixGov" was set up for collaborative writing on reform of government and continued for over two years, ending with publication early in 2003. Many of the participants came from another forum called Alternate Culture, and quite a few had responded to an invitation at Blue Ear Forum, largely composed of journalists and writers from around the world.

The purpose was stated on the FixGov home page as follows:

Fixing Government: FixGov aims to promote economic, ecological, and social justice. We are working on a book about government reform and we hope for ideas from many areas of the world.

The FixGov group exists because all the efforts individuals make for sustainable living can be offset by corporate and government decisions. How can local, national, and international governments be made answerable to the people they govern instead of just the power elites? When major polluters of the atmosphere use political muscle to escape environmental controls, what can be done by the people who have to breathe the polluted air? When municipal sewage dumping or industrial waste fouls water that is vital to human health, how can people protect themselves? When large-scale corporate agriculture and food processing distribute contaminated food and make consumers unknowing guinea pigs for genetic modification, radiation, and dangerous substances, how can they be subjected to effective control?

Join a discussion seeking ways to overcome the corruption that undermines public interest throughout the world, overthrowing or blocking democracy in some countries, making voting seem futile to many in the US, and secretly controlling such UN agencies as WTO, IMF, and the World Bank.

Please make a strong effort to base your comments on facts and remember to respect the comments of others, as your postings will go straight through without screening by a moderator.

Some 70 people joined in this project, including members from the United States, Canada, Mexico, United Kingdom, Netherlands, Poland, Sweden, India, Pakistan, Bangladesh, Mali, Australia, New Zealand, and possibly other countries (because email addresses do not always indicate the country). Messages were exchanged in English.

As members contributed their thoughts, a volunteer editor was sought. When nobody offered to take on the task, the founders inquired whether one of the particularly articulate participants, Adriaan Boiten, would be willing to assume the responsibility. He agreed, and in addition created a web site displaying the results of the discussion and links to appropriate sources. That web site can now be found at www.fixgov.org or www.fixgov.com and is maintained by another volunteer, James McGuigan.

At the beginning the discussion on the forum was wide-ranging and random. A difference in emphasis emerged between those whose main concern was developing more democratic structures in existing governmental units and others who saw more hope in small autonomous communities living in harmony with nature and sending representatives to bodies that would work out means of cooperation on a larger scale. Both approaches are reflected in the resulting book.

As editor, Adriaan Boiten defined the major topics around which the discussion continued. Each of the chapters is based on the work of a volunteer who summarized the consensus developed in discussions of the forum on one of the topics. These summaries were disseminated to the entire group, then revised in the light of comments received. Finally, they were embodied in this book, edited jointly by Adriaan Boiten and Richard Stimson. Any royalties received from this work will be used to further the objectives of the forum.

As in any forum, some people participated to a greater degree than others, but all were able to offer their thoughts and comment on the contributions of others. Any objections or disagreements were taken into account when the consensus reports were written. The most extensive work was done by the volunteers who prepared those reports. Their backgrounds are quite diverse.

Adriaan Boiten, co-editor, engaged in historical preservation for the City of Amsterdam for 12 years. He studied new and theoretical history at the Municipal University of Amsterdam, graduating in 1986, and performed civic service in the library of the International Institute of Social History in lieu of military service. As the proprietor of a web design business he lives and works in the old inner city of Amsterdam.

Richard Stimson, co-editor, is an author and retired business professor in High Point, North Carolina, serving voluntarily as national coordinator of the worldwide International Simultaneous Policy Organisation. Educated at Yale, Florida International University, and the University of North Carolina at Chapel Hill, his careers have spanned association management, public relations, university teaching, and computer operations.

James McGuigan in England, who set up www.fixgov.org, is working on the Earth Emergency Initiative (www.earthemergency.org) and World Future Council Initiative (www.worldfuturecouncil.org). He is also a webmaster and a computer programmer, currently obtaining his degree on Information Technology with the Open University. He is an avid contributor of articles to internet forums on a diverse range of subjects.

Peter Scott of New Zealand has contributed ideas for improvement of the layout design of the book.

James Hall, summarizer of the consensus on political systems, grew up in a family of Republicans, supported Barry Goldwater's presidential campaign and the Vietnam war, but gradually migrated to a liberal viewpoint. A long-time resident of Orlando, Florida, he worked 23 years for the Walt Disney Company in jobs from ride operator to technical writer. In the Transportation/Communications Union at Disney, he served as a shop steward, district trustee, and finally as President and Treasurer, representing the interests of 3,000 Disney employees. He also was a writer and editor of the union's district newsletter for nine years. With a master's degree in liberal studies, he has taught at community college, written for The American Partisan and several other web magazines, and is collaborating on a book with Ian Foster.

Liane Casten, who (with Stimson) assembled most of the material in the chapter on communications media, is an author, journalist, film writer and director. Presently she is co-founder and president of Chicago Media Watch, a volunteer watchdog group that monitors the media for bias, distortions and omissions, and she is working on her second book, an exposé of a criminal corporation. Her first book, Breast Cancer: Poisons, Profits and Prevention (Common Courage Press, 1996), grew out of a cover story in Ms. on the environmental connection to the disease. Her articles have also been published in E Magazine, The Nation, Mother Jones, Environment Health Perspectives, In These Times, Business Ethics, The Chicago Tribune and the Chicago Sun-Times. She wrote four documentary films and directed one of them. With an M.A. from the University of Chicago, she has also taught high school and college classes.

Richard Gauthier, who reported the consensus for the chapter on "The Spiritual Basis for Sustainable Living," was born in New Jersey, but has been living in Europe since 1986 as a yoga and meditation teacher. In the past five years he has worked in Poland on non-profit projects to spread organic farming in Poland and protect small farmers regarding Poland's pending membership in the European Union. As a member of the Ananda Marga yoga meditation association, founded by P. R. Sarkar (who died in 1990), he made several visits to India, became a monk and an authority on Sarkar's concept of Microvita. The organization was banned in India and its members blacklisted for its anti-capitalist, anti-communist socioeconomic philosophy, its anti-corruption stand, and a trumped-up murder charge against Sarkar later dismissed in court. To obtain a visa to enter India he changed his name legally from Richard F. Gauthier and got a new passport as Richard Richardson. He has also been known as Rudreshananda in India, and has the spiritual name of Viveka. Author of a book and many articles about Microvita, he runs several e-mail lists on various spiritual and scientific topics and can be reached at richard@sfo.pl

William N. "Bill" Ellis, summarizer of the chapters on civil society and on education, is a physicist, futurist, farmer working from the home he was born in on his farm in Rangeley, Maine, USA, to bring social change and civil globalization. He is General Coordinator of TRANET transnational network (tranet@rangeley.org) and of A Coalition for Self-Learning, that has recently published the book, "Creating Learning Communities," which grew out of his 1998 E. F. Schumacher Lecture in which he used homeschooling as an example of the application of chaos, complexity, and gaian theories in the social sphere. In the same lecture he used GrassRoots Organizations (GROs) as subset of Non-Governmental Organizations (NGOs) as another example of leaderless, unplanned, undesigned self-organization and speculated that the phenomenal growth and linking of GROs could lead to a radically different form of world governance.

1

Global Problems in Need of Solution

Global communication is good; global monopoly is bad. Worrying about global problems may seem unnecessary to those among us who are fortunate enough to be living in a democracy during a period of history that lacks many of the horrors of the past. Human sacrifice, cannibalism, slavery, colonial oppression, and many diseases are largely (but not entirely) behind us, as are two world wars, and it is right to be thankful for the benefits we have.

Laborsaving inventions of the Industrial Revolution have saved many of us from the backbreaking tasks of earlier times. The electronic age has made it possible to exchange information and ideas rapidly around the globe. Most innovation (although aided by government-funded research and sometimes subsidies) has been introduced to the public by private enterprise.

Yet there are serious problems, especially as the means now exist to destroy all humans on the planet, possibly by global climate change and certainly with weapons of mass destruction. Too often governments act in concert with armaments manufacturers to promote the sale of weapons of war, sometimes to both sides in a conflict. As an example, the foreign aid budget of the United States currently includes many times as much "military aid" as peaceful grants.

In the movement for sustainable development, groups of people have tried to escape from multinational corporate tyranny by forming self-sustaining communities, often drawing on the wisdom of indigenous cultures. These efforts for sustainable living, however, can be off-set by corporate and government decisions, as in the case of native populations driven off their lands by mining and drilling operations that have poisoned their water supplies and crops.

As the world becomes more interconnected, the reins of control are found in fewer hands and most people discover they have less control over their lives. History has known centralized power before, but the rise of democracy in the 19th and 20th centuries raised the hope of greater personal freedom under governments answerable to their citizenry.

Now this has often degenerated into what some call pseudo-democracy. Many people feel their choice in voting is between Tweedledum and Tweedledee, and so there are widespread protests and demonstrations, including some elements that become violent. Even some outbreaks of terrorism have their roots in the despair of people who have lost hope in peaceful solutions.

The tribal rivalries and centuries-old feuds between ancient enemies are made worse by irresponsible divide-and-conquer tactics of the great powers and marketing of armaments to both sides in each dispute, including proliferation of nuclear, chemical, and biological weapons of mass destruction.

When the most powerful people in the world come together in official economic conferences (G-8, IMF, WTO, etc.) and such unofficial groups as the Bilderberg, the Trilateral Commission, and the Council on Foreign Relations, they remain in splendid isolation from the less powerful people. After a series of protest demonstrations at major cities, they have recently held their official meetings behind strong barricades and heavily armed police forces and/or at isolated locations.

The emphasis is on economic growth, but the measures they use are badly flawed. Gross domestic product (GDP) is based entirely on money transactions, thus missing the value of housework, home cooking, child raising, do-it-yourself work at home, "sweat equity," and all forms of voluntary service. Robert Eisner's 1994 book,

The Misunderstood Economy, asked: "If restaurant meals are substituted for home cooking, is that an increase in product?" He estimated conservatively that if the value of unpaid labor services in the home were included the 1992 U.S. GDP would have been $8 trillion instead of $6 trillion. On the other hand, GDP ignores economic harm done to nature and to the health of individuals.

Prominent at these meetings are top bankers, financiers, corporate executives, media owners, and politicians. Hardly ever present are labor leaders, consumer representatives, or environmentalists. Secrecy results in rumors of plots for world control that are sometimes wild and sometimes not totally outlandish.

There are indications that the globalization moves and "neo-liberal" economics of these organizations have led to increasing disparity of wealth and income both within and between nations. In short, it is held that the rich are getting richer and the poor are getting poorer. Details of this disparity in wealth and income are given in Chapter 4.

A June 2002 report of the UN Conference on Trade and Development (UNCTAD) on the poverty trap of less developed countries investigated "whether the current form of globalization is tightening the poverty trap and also increasing the vulnerabilities of those countries that appear to be escaping it." The answer was, in effect, "Yes." The report, however, stopped short of admitting that World Bank, IMF, etc., are collaborating with multinational corporations to bring about the impoverishment described in the report. (www.unctad.org)

The specific problems that are described in the chapters on political systems, corporate power, monetary systems, and the communications media are very closely interrelated—and also interwoven with concerns about education, justice, medicine, religious freedom, land use, the oceans, and the atmosphere.

Aids to their solution are presented in the chapters on spirituality, alternative life styles, and education. Proposed solutions are summarized in the final chapter of conclusions.

The discussion addresses how local, national, and international governments can be made answerable to the people they govern instead of just the power elites. The goal is to make globalization work for the benefit of people and the environment instead of "neo-liberal" globalization of the "wild west" variety that has spread poverty, financial crisis, desperation, and bloodshed in many parts of the world that have become more and more unstable.

2

Perfecting Democracy in Political Systems

✦

(based on a summary by James Hall in Orlando, Florida)

This chapter notes the spread of democratic elections as the basis for governance in more countries of the world, although imperfections exist even in the best of democracies. The forces that concentrate wealth and power into a few hands, and that abuse the earth's environment for their own benefit, also oppose democratic reforms, social justice, human rights, and efforts to create a sustainable local economy. Ways of overcoming these obstacles and furthering genuine democracy are discussed. A "security state" of the closed, fundamentalist, and ruthless variety is not the solution for public fears and needs generated by terrorism.

Although many people would like to conduct their personal, family, and community lives without interference from government, that is not the way it is. Even remote parts of the world are coming under political control, often combined with invasion by economic power. Thus traditional cultures in areas as widespread as Nigeria, Brazil, Papua New Guinea, and elsewhere are being driven off their land by the combined actions of governments and foreign exploiting industries, including cyanide or oil spills in their streams, destruction of their crops, and repressive police action.

There is a legitimate difference of opinion as to how much or little government is desirable, but the alternative to government—anarchy—has not been demonstrated to work well in a world where greed overpowers goodwill. That makes it important what kind of government we have. Anarchy requires an educated and empowered independent public to work properly. It is never in the best interests of hierarchies to allow these conditions to exist in reality.

Although it is often far from perfect in practice, democracy operates on the principle that no leader can be trusted to know what people need and want better than the people themselves. It aims to meet the desires of the majority without being unfair to minorities.

Those who are lucky live in one of the world's liberal democracies where generally (if not perfectly) leaders are elected by popular vote and human rights are honored. Since 1950, the world has seen a phenomenal growth of democracies, from 22 nations representing 31% of the world's population, to 120 electoral democracies representing 58% of the world's people.

That's a shift of historic importance, but it's not enough. Seventy-two sovereign nations representing 42% of the world's people still have no representative government. In such nations, working for democracy is an important first step towards creating social justice and a sustainable world economy. Some countries may have a democratically elected government, but few recognized human rights, and in some democracy and human rights may rest on fragile foundations.

Even members of long-established democracies can't rest but must work hard to keep elections honest and citizens' rights from being abused. There are powerful interests that benefit from restricting human rights and corrupting democratic institutions.

There was a time, perhaps, when politics was a noble statecraft and politicians were regarded in high esteem. Politics was not their profession; they came from various respectable professional backgrounds; such as lawyers, physicians, teachers, landlords etc. Politicians belonging to a party believed in the ideology for which the party stood, and dedicated themselves to fulfilling the party objectives. Today politics is a full time profession to most politicians.

The forces that concentrate wealth and power into a few hands and that abuse the earth's environment for their own benefit oppose democratic reforms, social justice, human rights, and efforts to create a sustainable local economy. Their goal is to block genuine democratic institutions, manipulate elections, limit human rights, and use the environment for their shortsighted interest—to gain wealth and hold onto power.

A good citizen's political work is never done, and he or she must be vigilant both to create a better world and to sustain it. Corruption can occur both in the electoral process and in unfair influencing of public officials that amounts to bribery although not always illegal.

For example, *The Buying of Congress* by Charles Lewis and the Center for Public Integrity (Avon Books, 1998) reports that in the United States thousands die and millions become ill from poisoned foods. Meanwhile Congress has blocked tougher safety standards and received $40 million campaign donations in ten years from the food industry.

Also, members of Congress received $180 million from the 500 largest corporations and cut corporate income tax rates to provide only 10% of all federal revenue compared with 28% in 1956. With great difficulty a bill was passed in 2002 that may make a start on campaign finance reform if it withstands court challenges.

The light of world public opinion has brought about honest elections in many countries for the first time with the help in some cases of United Nations monitors and in other cases of impartial international observers organized by former U.S. president Jimmy Carter.

Any nation dominated by just one party fails to function as a democratic system. Some regimes try to give the appearance of democracy, but if only one party is permitted, the elections are mere window-dressing. The same is true in a two-party system when the same powerful interests largely control both parties. New parties should not face unreasonable requirements to get on the ballot. Legitimate voters should not be hindered and fraudulent voting should be prevented.

The method of recording and counting votes varies among democratic countries, and there are advocates for each system. Balloting methods range from paper ballots marked with party symbols for the illiterate to high-tech mechanical or electronic voting machines. Honest counts require that there be a way to recheck the votes, so paper ballots must be safeguarded and machine tallies must preserve an audit trail so that totals can be checked against individual votes.

Some elections are conducted on a "winner-take-all" basis where the candidate with the most votes in his or her district is elected. An alternative is proportional representation where each party gets the number of seats in a representative body that is in proportion to the votes it got in the election. In some jurisdictions, if a candidate fails to receive a majority of the votes cast, a run-off election is held between the two highest scoring candidates. Preference voting, or "instant run-off," is sometimes used where voters record first, second, and maybe third choices, for example, which are counted in order until someone has a majority.

The U.S. presidential election involves an indirect method in which members of an "Electoral College" are chosen on the basis of whom they are pledged to support and then they choose the president (and vice president). Most states allocate all their electoral votes to the party that scored highest. Usually this results in choosing a president who also received the highest national popular vote, but there have been four exceptions, including George W. Bush in 2000, who was chosen by a difference of 537 votes in one state.

Variations in these methods can be quite acceptable, so long as they are approved by those governed and reflect the will of the people. Choices made by politicians, however, often suit their own personal and party interests. One of their tricks is to lay out districts (constituencies) for party advantage. This is called "gerrymandering" for an

American politician named Gerry who mapped a district in the shape of a salamander.

Officials, once elected, can be subverted in various ways. Corporations increasingly are using favors to politicians in ways that are tantamount to bribes, although they may not meet the legal definition of a crime. Even judges receive benefits that interfere with their objectivity. Corporations in the United States, and organizations heavily financed by them, have entertained at least 600 federal judges at luxury resort locations for seminars where they are exposed to propaganda for a pro-business movement called Law and Economics.

Corporations have also spent millions to sponsor research and endow professorships reinforcing their points of view in law schools and other areas of academic study, notably including economics. Since the creation of NAFTA and WTO (see Chapter 3), they have used clauses banning trade restrictions to sue against national and local laws designed to protect health, safety, and the environment. Through the World Bank and IMF (see Chapters 3 and 4) they have obtained control of government-owned telephone systems, water supplies, and other public utilities, to privatize them for private profit, as well as drilling and mining to the detriment of local farmers and fishermen.

National and local governments find themselves forced to compete against each other to attract industry by offering subsidies and repeal of public interest laws and regulations. One proposed method of forcing multinational corporations to "play by the rules" is the concept of "Simultaneous Policy" explained in a book of that name by John Bunzl. It suggests that political parties could be induced to pledge that when they are in power, and when most other nations have similarly pledged, the nations will simultaneously enact measures for such control of international finance and industry as individual nations were unable to do on their own.

The International Simultaneous Policy Organisation (ISPO) is working toward that end in more than 20 countries (www.simpol.org).

Among its objectives is the democratizing of such international agencies as the World Bank, IMF, WTO, etc.

The World Federalist Association (www.wfa.org) and the Campaign for UN Reform (www.cunr.org) work for strengthening and reforming the United Nations. Despite the accomplishments of the UN, it also needs to be made more democratic and responsible to the world's people. Any higher level of government needs to be carefully limited in its scope and kept under democratic control to preclude the creation of a global tyranny.

A further problem that complicates efforts for worldwide peace and freedom is the desire of some groups to establish a separate national homeland. This involves taking over land occupied by someone else and/or seceding from an existing government that usually wants to keep control. Hostilities can result with participants being labeled "freedom fighters" by one side and "terrorists" by the other. Under ideal conditions, each nation would be inhabited only by people who willingly consent to being under the government, which in turn would guarantee the rights and freedom of all. That is obviously a very long-term objective, but taking steps in that direction is imperative, both for the good of the contenders and for the welfare of the whole world in the context of weapons of mass destruction.

Despite general agreement on most of the points in this chapter, there are some people who feel that political systems are so corrupt that it is useless to vote. They prefer to arrange their own lives in a way they think will be beneficial to people and the environment and to encourage others to do likewise.

Voting percentages have declined sharply in many countries, partly because of a cynical feeling that "my vote won't make any difference," and partly because commercial media have encouraged later generations to focus on entertainment, trivia, and self-gratification. In a few countries, voting is legally required. This, it can be argued, is an invasion of freedom. If voting is to enable everyone to make choices, it should include the choice of not voting. Some have suggested a choice on the ballot should be "none of the above" with the election to be declared invalid _f that choice wins.

While some believe that progress lies in adopting different lifestyles and community organizations (which can certainly be beneficial), the freedom to pursue these and other personal choices seems to require reform of the powerful structures that limit freedom. The many sacrifices of those who died to replace despotism with democracy, and the eagerness of newly enfranchised citizens of former tyrannies to exercise their voting rights despite all obstacles, are arguments against abandoning one's right to vote.

Global domination by corporate cartels has had detrimental effects on both the more powerful and less powerful countries. Arms sales have fueled internal warfare in less developed countries. The destruction of indigenous environments plus concentration of unemployed and homeless people in cities, combined with repressive governments in league with the multinational corporations (mining, oil, and timber companies) has generated waves of migration for economic and political reasons.

As developed countries have been overrun by immigrants, often seeking asylum, cultural clashes and competition for jobs have had their effects. For example, European social-democratic or center-left governments, which have been under pressure from private business to reduce their social services and worker protections, are finding that new issues are arising. The traditional supporters of those parties see their social protections deteriorating while immigrants seek to share the benefits.

Immigration and integration are now at the top of the political agenda in Europe, which is sad for all those who are engaged in rational discussions. There are real social and economic reasons for existing tensions, but culture becomes more or less the platform on which people can express their frustrations and emotions, feeling patriotic.

New opposition arises to parties that are seen to be patronizing, arrogant, bureaucratic, and "politically correct." Voters turn to parties that promise action on the new issues that concern them, such as street crime and threats by Islamic fundamentalism against traditional liberal values. People don't trust the professional politicians any more in London, Paris, or The Hague. In Holland, for example, the last 5-10 years saw the rise of countless local parties that won local elections with local issues, feeding on fear of street crime and outrage about bureaucratic decisions of the local councils.

The localization of politics could be furthered by Information and Communication Technology (ICT), especially through the Internet, which makes it easier for localities to be more independent from the knowledge and power centers. People become better informed, communicate via the web, organize themselves in discussion groups, meet each other, and start to move. The possibility for people to work at home instead of travelling to the city can make them more independent and capable of participating in self-government.

Suggestions for action:

If some of these suggestions are impossible under your form of government, consider them as goals to be reached, and work to change the political circumstances so that you have the right as a citizen to exercise them.

1. Work to advance social justice, democracy, and environmentally sound policies.

2. Work against concentration of wealth and power into a few hands—whether in the name of good or ill—and against pollution or waste the earth's resources.

3. Block efforts of those who would subvert democracy by organizing opposition; educating others and demonstrating against wrongs; taking legal action to enforce human rights.

4. Vote at every opportunity: check out candidates' records, join a political party or create one to reflect your values, volunteer to help candidates write letters for publication attend meetings and express your concerns, donate time and money if you can.

5. Help keep your political system honest: work as a poll-watcher and monitor the counting of ballots, help those who are illiterate to read their ballots, support efforts to keep balloting both secret and honest.

6. Become involved in local community organizations that reflect your agenda, work with local people to clean up your local environment, to create more parks and people-friendly environments, to support public transportation, to protect civil rights, to elect responsible local and national officials, and to fight pollution and unwanted corporate intrusion; work to educate your community through letters, newsletters, organized events, and demonstrations.

7. Encourage cooperation by your local groups with other local, regional, national and international organizations. Support candidates and parties that advance your efforts and work for positive changes.

8. Work for:

- the creation of constitutional, democratic institutions;

- the non-violent resolution of conflicts;

- basic human rights for all people;

- environmental protections that sustain local ecosystems;

- recycling of wastes;

- alternative energy sources;

- environmentally appropriate building technologies; habitat and species restoration.

- effective monitoring of ecosystems;

- sustainable local agriculture;

- voter initiatives that can bypass representative bodies and place issues directly before the voters;

- open government, including keeping all meetings and records public and "transparent" subject to the public's scrutiny and criticism;

- public financing of political campaigns to keep money from "special interests" from having an impact on the government's ability to do the people's work;

- media (press, radio, television, web access, etc.) free of control by government or corporate monopolies but required to broadcast candidate debates and political forums in the public interest;

- democratic regulation of all private use of the "public commons," including air, water, public parkland, etc.

- "true-costing" of any products or industrial processes that might cause environmental degradation, including in their costs the regulation and clean-up of any pollution, and use of those costs to perform the cleanup;

- creation of agencies to monitor the environment, detect pollution and polluters, and to charge and fine them the amount needed to cleanup any resulting pollution;

- redefinition of the legal status of the corporation (see Chapter 3);

- promotion of democratic, transparent international organizations to replace current institutions like the World Bank, WTO, and IMF.

- When considering reforms to correct global abuses, it should not be forgotten that votes can be registered in the marketplace and not just at the polling place. Some organizations have had success with boycotts of offending companies to bring changes in their behavior. The choices of consumers can have considerable effect on the degree of pollution and waste of natural resources resulting from production. To accomplish favorable results, they must resist advertising and promotion of inefficient, wasteful, and unnecessary products.

"If liberty and equality, as is thought by some are chiefly to be found in democracy, they will be best attained when all persons alike share in the government to the utmost."

—Aristotle (384 BC–322 BC)

"It has been said that democracy is the worst form of government except all the others that have been tried."

—Sir Winston Churchill (1874–1965)

3

Restoring Human Control over Corporate Power

"Corporations rule," says the *Hightower Lowdown* newsletter. "No other institution comes close to matching the power that the 500 biggest corporations have amassed over us. The clout of all 535 members of [the U.S.] Congress is nothing compared to the individual and collective power of these predatory behemoths that now roam the globe, working their will over all competing interests.

"The aloof and pampered executives who run today's autocratic and secretive corporate states have effectively become our sovereigns. From who gets health care to who pays taxes, from what's on the news to what's in our food, they have usurped the people's democratic authority and now make these broad social decisions in private, based solely on the interests of their corporations." The quoted paragraphs introduced an April 2002 exposé of the world's biggest corporation, Wal-Mart, with more than $220 billion annual revenues (www.jimhightower.com).

The compensation of chief executive officers of these corporations (CEOs) in the United States by 2001 averaged 531 times that of blue-collar workers compared with a 40 to 1 ratio in 1960. The highest rewards went to those who had fired workers and found tax loopholes for their companies, according to "Executive Excess 2001," Institute for Policy Studies and United for a Fair Economy (*Multinational Monitor*, Oct. 2001, p. 4).

Some, but not all, of the world's wealthiest people are CEOs—others exert their control behind the scenes as major stockholders or financial backers. Corporate management, directors, investment advisors, stockbrokers, bankers, lawyers, and accountants are supposed to be looking after the interests of the stockholders. Often they seem to be more concerned with personal profits to be made from trading in and out, fees, commissions, stock options, and all the other gimmicks for their own benefit. They "scratch each others backs" and "one hand washes another." Ordinary investors are lucky to have their interests get any consideration. Their ownership through mutual funds and/or pension plans is routinely used by the trustees (without consulting them) to rubber-stamp management proposals.

Extreme abuses in some corporations came to light in 2002, when one of the world's biggest accounting firms, Arthur Andersen, was convicted of obstruction of justice in the case of Enron. This involved one of the world's largest corporations where members of top management walked away with millions of dollars from the company plus large profits from selling Enron stock before declaring bankruptcy.

The Andersen firm provided advice to set up undisclosed partnerships for hiding corporate losses, and simultaneously served as auditors to verify the reliability of the company's financial reports. Employee pension funds invested in Enron stock were almost completely wiped out, as was the value of stock bought by small investors trusting financial analysts and stock brokers.

Although Enron had been rated at or near the top of all corporations based on the market value of its stock, it owned very few physical assets. It was described as an energy trader, and its manipulations were discovered to have been behind the electric power crisis in California. Other activities included buying public utilities, including water supply services, from governments around the world at bargain prices and then jacking up the rates to customers of the privatized monopoly. It was among the largest donors of campaign contributions to politicians—tantamount to bribes, if not legally so defined.

While investigations and litigation involving Enron were still going on, another Arthur Anderson client, WorldCom, disclosed the largest corporate overstatement of cash flow in history, amounting to more than $3.8 billion in the previous 15 months, using a series of accounting tricks to hide expenses and inflate cash flow. The company's CEO owed the company more than $366 million for loans and loan guarantees when he abruptly resigned, the stock that had sold for $62 dropped to about 9 cents, and 17,000 workers were to lose their jobs.

Only a week earlier, executives of Rite Aid, a drug store chain, were indicted, having run up a record overstatement of profits totaling $2.3 billion over two years. This company's auditor was another large accounting firm, KPMG. Other recent corporate scandals include Global Crossing (an Andersen client) and Tyco. Merrill Lynch and other brokerage firms were found to have been urging customers to buy stock in such companies that the analysts knew were in trouble.

Multinational corporations have close ties to major financial houses, which will be discussed further in the next chapter. Directors of banks, investment companies, and other corporations serve on each other's boards and they or their representatives are appointed official advisors to governments. They employ former government officials as lobbyists, who then may return to prominent government positions in a process sometimes known as the "revolving door." Armament companies put retired generals and admirals on their boards of directors, while top executives move in an out of high-level government jobs.

Those munitions manufacturers, preferring to be called "defense industries," also are major financial supporters of politicians, resulting in getting not only government contracts but also subsidies and help in selling their products to foreign countries. A report by the Congressional Research Service in 2000 disclosed that the United States is the world's leading arms merchant, responsible for almost half the weapons sold worldwide, 70% going to developing countries. Listed next in order as suppliers were Russia, France, Germany, Britain, China, and Italy.

Aside from threats of nuclear war and terrorist attacks, the major challenge to democracy and human progress involves the domination by corporations of the institutions of self-government, which is made more difficult when the corporations are actually bigger than the national governments. Democracy has always had an uphill fight against various forms of tyranny, whether absolute monarchies or military dictatorships.

Through concentrated corporate control of the information media, as well as corporate favors and campaign financing to politicians, the rulers of big corporations tend to get their way most of the time. On the world scene, global corporations (including global bankers and financial companies) dominate international agencies unrestrained by democratic safeguards.

A network of faceless bureaucracies, the most familiar of which are the World Bank, the International Monetary Fund (IMF), and the World Trade Organization (WTO), make no pretense of being democratic and are dominated by representatives from large transnational corporations and banks.

Already, both the USA and the European Union (EU) have been compelled by the WTO to annul various of their health and environmental laws. Most of the third world has been forced to adopt entire legislative agendas dictated by the IMF under what are called "free trade" treaties, and under conditions which are attached to loans given to third-world countries by the regime's agencies.

The governments, in some cases, have made deals with multinational corporations to share in profits from mining operations that drive native populations off their lands either by using military force or by contaminating their sources of livelihood, resulting in cities crowded with unemployed, homeless adults and children.

Under pressure from the global bankers to attract foreign investors, governments have suppressed labor unions and held down wages, benefits, and labor standards. They have given special tax breaks to foreign corporations and relaxed environmental regulation. Recently they have been required to raise water prices and then sell government water utilities to private monopolies ("Privatization Tidal Wave: IMF/World Bank Water Policies and the Price Paid by the Poor" by Sara Grusky, *Multinational Monitor*, Sept. 2001).

Nations have also allowed misuse of patent laws. Corporations send representatives, sometimes called "bio-pirates," to learn from indigenous people about natural remedies. Then the companies apply for patents to turn these remedies into profitable monopolies. Patents have even been awarded for genes and other natural phenomena that corporations have identified or "discovered" in their laboratories.

A study of World Bank and IMF loan documents with 26 countries shows that they require privatizing of government-owned enterprises, layoffs of government employees, easing of rules on firings and working conditions, increasing the wage gap between employees and managers, and cutting pensions for workers.

For example, the World Bank recommended to Vicente Fox when his new government came into power in Mexico that there be a phase-out of severance payments, collective bargaining, enforceable labor contracts, seniority rules, and liability for subcontractors' employees. It also has stated that it cannot support workers' freedom of association and right to collective bargaining. ("Against the Workers: How IMF and World Bank Policies Undermine Labor Power and Rights" by Vincent Lloyd and Robert Weissman, *Multinational Monitor*, Sept. 2001.)

A few examples from around the world will illustrate the unfortunate results. In Haiti, after the military dictatorship was removed from power and the elected president Aristide returned with U.S. help, the IMF, the World Bank, the U.S. Agency for International Development, and the Inter-American Development Bank offered to help Haiti rebuild. However, the economic program they imposed was the so-called "neo-liberal" structural adjustment that bankers have favored around the world.

Similar plans forced on Haiti's neighbors—Mexico, Nicaragua, and Venezuela—were supposed to reduce poverty and external debts. Instead they widened the income gap, increased poverty, and undermined national sovereignty. These conditions involved privatization of state-owned industries, deregulation of the economy, and opening the country to massive foreign investment.

Costa Rica has long been known as one of the most democratic of Latin American countries, with less of an income gap than its neighbors. The IMF and the World Bank have begun to change this, ostensibly to pay off foreign debt. Thousands of small farmers have been displaced in favor of large agricultural export operations. Increasing crime and violence have resulted in higher police costs, and the country now imports its basic food requirements. Although foreign debt has doubled, Costa Rica has been able to meet its debt service payments, so the IMF and the World Bank call it a success story.

The World Bank, which awarded Mexico 13 structural and sectoral adjustment loans between 1980 and 1991, imposed the following conditions on its 1991 agricultural loan: slashing tariffs, canceling price controls on basic foods, privatizing state-owned monopolies, and eliminating price guarantees for corn—the mainstay of the rural poor.

A million people died in Mozambique, a Cold War hot spot where rebel forces backed by apartheid South Africa and right-wing U.S. business with covert U.S. government approval fought the left-wing movement that took over the government after Portugal pulled out. The U.S. forced Mozambique to join the IMF and World Bank in 1984, which resulted in World Bank-mandated "structural adjustment" in 1987, and an IMF-controlled stabilization" in 1990.

The World Bank used many loans in the 1950s in an effort to win India away from policies of building local production to displace imports and of government intervention in the economy. Large-scale development projects have displaced 20 million people over a 40-year period. After the World Bank withheld $750 million in Indian energy loans to enforce compliance with its opposition to the government program for electrification in rural areas, the Indian government scaled back alternative energy subsidies and power projects in its poorest states.

The fastest growing component of the World Bank is now the International Finance Corporation (IFC) which loans directly to private companies, including multinational corporations, such as Chase, Citibank, Sumitomo Bank, New York Life, DuPont, Daimler-Chrysler, Electricité de France, Portugal Telecom, Shell, etc. Simultaneously, governments are pressured to turn over public utilities to such private companies. ("Dubious Development: The World Bank's Foray Into Private Sector Investment" by Charlie Cray, *Multinational Monitor*, September 2001; www.essential.org/monitor)

When the North American Free Trade Agreement (NAFTA) was negotiated, certain externalities were supposed to be covered by "side agreements" on workers rights and the environment, but subsequent events showed the agreements to be toothless. The greatest harm was in the failure of protections against pollution and labor exploitation. As reported in a 1996 article in *Dollars and Sense*, "Corporations and their government allies in all three NAFTA countries vehemently opposed setting up institutions with strong monitoring and enforcement powers." They had their way, as no budget was provided for enforcement. A proposed expansion of NAFTA to the whole Western Hemisphere as Free Trade Area of the Americas (FTAA) seems likely to offer the same empty promises.

The European Community or European Union (EU), on the other hand, consists of nations that are much more concerned about preventing the exploitation of labor and the environment than the NAFTA countries have been. National laws and EU rules, such as the Social Chapter, provide a framework within which corporations must operate, however grudgingly. The biggest corporations and political parties friendly to them keep trying to relax such rules.

One of the first attempts to bring corporations under control occurred in Europe on May 30, 2002, according to a news release issued by Richard Howitt, European Parliament Rapporteur (Spokes-person) on Corporate Social Responsibility. The European Parliament in Brussels voted for new legislation to require companies to publicly report annually on their social and environmental performance, to make board members personally responsible for these practices, and to establish legal jurisdiction against European companies' abuses in developing countries.

In Europe social-democratic parties have been trying a "Third Way" between corporate freedom and social responsibility. They set out to reform the welfare state, sometimes (as in The Netherlands, Belgium, and France) together with moderate Liberal politicians (that is, in European terminology, those favoring corporate freedom).

This led to great disenchantment among the population, who saw private wealth grow while public wealth and security dwindled. European people want to be protected against overwhelming economic power by a social-democratic state, but the politicians weakened government in favor of the market.

Paradoxically, the extreme right-wing politicians in Europe, who want a strong state to close the borders against immigrants and proclaim jingoistic values, now tend to be the only parties giving people some sense of active government. Corporate power over the people—without responsible social government—leads not only to despair and terrorism in the Third World, but also to a boost for political fascism in Europe.

People feel helpless against the economy and seek for scapegoats for their disenchantment, rising crime, and economic volatility. There is a grave danger now of a link between private corporate power and the emerging extreme-right parties. These parties blame the usual scapegoats, such as immigrants and Jews, for social problems actually due to global oligarchy and thus shift attention away from the real causes.

Franklin D. Roosevelt said: "The liberty of a democracy is not safe if the people tolerate the growth of private power to a point where it becomes stronger than their democratic State itself. That, in its essence, is Fascism—ownership of government by an individual, by a group or any controlling private power."

Instead of listening to the people, European Social Democrats, like corporations, have relied on marketing techniques to sell their policies. They are now paying the price for leaving Europe open to uncontrolled corporate power and unreformed globalization. It is in the interest of believers in democracy all over the world to strengthen rational, democratic structures, expanding them into the corporate world, and thus to give people their power back.

Apart from corporate domination of many aspects of government, the structure of the work environment imposed by large corporations has serious effects on family and community life. The past few decades have seen changes that reduce the time people have for activities outside the workplace environment, although taking different form in three areas: the United States, Europe, and less developed areas.

The expansion of work by women outside the home has been widespread. To the extent it represents more options open to women this can be counted as progress. However, for many women the option of remaining at home to care for children has largely been foreclosed by economic necessity.

Longer working hours have been required by employers where unions and government protections are weak, particularly in the sweatshops of less developed countries, where people have been forced off their land to form a labor pool in the cities and where child labor is common. Employers in the United States extend the hours in some jobs to avoid hiring additional workers, which would entail the cost of fringe benefits such as health insurance, pension plans, unemployment insurance, etc. Conversely, employers make some other jobs part time—often about 37 hours per week—to avoid coverage for fringe benefits, but workers have to take more than one job to survive. Europe has been less affected, so far, by the trend for long hours, due to relatively stronger labor unions.

In most countries, including the U.S., corporations and their controlling stockholders tend to dominate politics despite any laws intended to prevent it. Corporations generally enjoy a favored status in the courts where they have the privileges of natural persons without the responsibilities. The limited liability of corporations allows their officers to escape financial and personal responsibility in many improper schemes such as the Enron scandal (where the final outcome for officers of the corporation and its auditors is yet to be seen). It is common for top officials to get reimbursement from the company for legal expense and fines whenever they are taken to court for their actions.

"In 1971, only 175 businesses had registered lobbyists in Washington. By 1988, 1,634 out of every 100,000 Washingtonians was a lawyer," according to *The Paradox of American Democracy, Elites, Special Interests, and the Betrayal of Public Trust* by John B. Judis. "By the mid-1980," writes Judis, "there were over a thousand former officials in Washington working as lobbyists, including over 200 former members of Congress…and much of what they were hired to do was to defeat environmental and social legislation which the corporations deem 'unaffordable'."

As governments began to abandon enforcement of antitrust laws, mergers and acquisitions placed more and more of the world's economy in fewer hands. Economies of scale are usually given as the reason for business combinations. For any business, efficiency tends to increase with size up to some point. Often this is interpreted as "the bigger the better." However, large units are not always more efficient, because the disadvantages of bureaucracy exist in private enterprise as well as government.

Many studies have shown that relatively small companies produce more innovation, new products, and new jobs than the giant corporations. The motivation for mergers and acquisitions, therefore, is more often a desire for market control than efficiency. Another motive, of course, has been the opportunity for windfalls to top management as well as Wall Street lawyers and investment bankers.

Adam Smith's "Wealth of Nations" explained how an "invisible hand" will cause the selfish actions of suppliers and consumers to create an equilibrium in the market that benefits everyone better than the mercantilist system (with its government monopolies) then existing. The book is revered by classical economists, but they often forget that his theory completely depends on really free competition and other basic assumptions about the market. Smith was aware of imperfections and declared in that book: "It is to prevent reduction of price...by restraining free competition...that all corporations, and the greater part of corporation laws, have been established."

The assumptions of classical economics on the Adam Smith model are seriously violated by Wal-Mart, which has become the world's largest corporation, surpassing Exxon-Mobil. In the *Hightower Lowdown* article cited at the beginning of this chapter, Wal-Mart is not only a scofflaw in its own labor practices but also presses its suppliers in China and other low-wage countries (whose names and locations it keeps secret) to drive down costs by cutting wages and benefits. The article continues:

"By slashing its retail prices way below cost when it enters a community, Wal-Mart can crush our groceries, pharmacies, hardware stores, and other retailers, then raise its prices once it has monopoly control over the market....By crushing local businesses, this giant eliminates three decent jobs for every two Wal-Mart jobs that it creates...."

Special characteristics of corporations under U.S. law that make them different from individuals include these:

1. Corporations have perpetual life.

2. Corporations can be in two or more places at the same time.

3. Corporations cannot be jailed.

4. Corporations pursue a single-minded goal, profit, and are typically legally prohibited from seeking other ends.

5. There are no limits, natural or otherwise, to corporations' potential size.

6. Because of their political power, they are able to define or, at very least, substantially affect the civil and criminal regulations that define the boundaries of permissible behavior. Virtually no individual criminal has such abilities.

7. Corporations can combine with each other, into bigger and more powerful entities.

8. Corporations can divide themselves, shedding subsidiaries or affiliates that are controversial, have brought them negative publicity, or pose liability threats.

These unique attributes give corporations extraordinary power, and makes the challenge of checking their power all the more difficult. The institutions are much more powerful than individuals, which makes all the more frightening their single-minded profit maximizing efforts.

(Adapted from "Corporations: Different Than You and Me" by Russell Mokhiber and Robert Weissman)

The power of the corporate oligarchy is displayed whenever there is an international meeting of such groups as the World Bank, International Monetary Fund (IMF), World Trade Organization (WTO), or the G-8 economic summit. The United States sends its CIA and FBI to work with local agencies to make sure the delegates are not bothered by, or exposed to, any public objections.

Peaceful protesters are regularly attacked with tear gas, water cannons, and charging hordes of police with helmets, shields, clubs, and firearms, using the excuse that somewhere vandals are rioting and looting—or else citing violence, when the violence was actually by the police or their *agents provocateurs*. Meanwhile, inside the fortified enclave the big corporations get what they want while defenders of the environment and human rights get mere lip service.

Despite the enormous power of the corporations and their friends in government, the role of corporations in the political process tends to be ignored by the academic community. According to Russell Mokhiber, editor of the *Corporate Crime Reporter* and Robert Weissman, editor of the *Multinational Monitor,* a recent convention of the American Political Science Association in Washington, D.C., almost entirely neglected corporate power in about a thousand papers presented.

Local, regional, and national governments compete for industrial development by offering subsidies, privileges, and tax breaks at the expense of the public and other businesses. By failing to enforce health and safety standards, they put the public at risk of disease, injury, and death, while allowing business to profit from polluting air, water, and food, including the use of people as unwilling guinea pigs for experiments with hormones, radiation, and genetic modification of food.

Politicians accept money from business interests to let them drive people off their land and poison it with petroleum spills, cyanide from gold mining, and other abuses. Corrupt national leaders hide their ill-gotten gains in secret foreign bank accounts, while using force to intimidate and kill opponents of exploitation by the multinational corporations. They side with business owners to destroy trade unions and prevent worker protests against unsafe working conditions.

Localities now compete for corporate headquarters and other enterprises by outright subsidies, tax abatements, and laws that favor employers against trade unions and unorganized workers. Similar practices are applied to competition for professional sports teams and even for the Olympic Games. In the same way, shipping companies have avoided national restrictions by chartering their vessels in countries like Panama and Liberia that have competed by offering permissive charters.

At the global level, the International Monetary Fund (IMF) acts to protect banks and speculators from losses due to bad judgment, while pressuring governments to curtail public services. The World Bank and the IMF place conditions on financial aid to developing countries that favor penetration by multinational corporations and curtailment of government protections for its citizens.

The World Trade Organization (WTO) makes decisions in secret, with almost never any involvement of nongovernmental organizations (NGOs). Industry representatives and government trade negotiators often closely allied with them denounce health, safety, and ethical rules of member states as unauthorized barriers to trade and impose penalties against countries that try to enforce these protections.

Information media (to be discussed in detail in another chapter) have largely been transformed into propaganda machines run either by repressive governments or by an oligarchy of corporations that control most of the media, as well as much of the world economy. The military-industrial complex manufactures weapons of mass destruction in ever larger numbers the making of which uses natural resources far surpassing those of the conventional market and increasingly places the world at risk of destruction.

In recent years corporations have been obtaining patents that would have been flatly rejected in the past. Outrageous copyright extensions will be discussed in the chapter on the media. Corporations have now been allowed to patent many innovations pioneered by government-conducted and/or government-financed research. Their friends in the U.S. Congress and Patent Office have allowed them to obtain patents on the products of nature (herbal remedies of indigenous peoples), genes of living creatures, and other things that are completely inappropriate to be patented. It also works out that individual inventors seldom get the financial benefit of their work, because their employers require them to sign over all their rights to the company.

Individual actions have little direct impact on government decision-making today. The deck is stacked against us and manipulated by corporate interests. The same holds true on environmental issues where the actions of individuals compared with those of corporations is miniscule, but the public is subjected to strict emissions testing while businesses continue polluting with use of political influence and delaying tactics.

Some governments have set up programs to pay corporations to become more energy and resource efficient, but sometimes this merely resulted in corporate welfare. Some large corporations have invested in efficiency measures and their return on investment was better than their investments in their product lines.

Among the reasons for corporation actions harmful to the environment is the economic system that ignores what economists call "externalities." That is, business activities may involve serious costs to others in the form of pollution-caused illnesses, poisoning of food sources (such as fish in the streams and crops in the land), and hazards to employees that do not enter into product costs and prices.

One suggested method of correcting this would be for government to require such costs to be included in prices, with proceeds to be used for overcoming the harmful effects. This is called "true-cost-pricing" and is further discussed in chapter 3 of Jim Bell's book, free at www.jimbell.com.

Some of the uncontrolled actions of major corporations are so heinous no monetary amount could compensate for the damage. At the top of the list might be sales of arms, often to both sides of conflicts. Here it is valuable for the armament manufacturers to have friends in government, both to obtain "defense" contracts and to arrange military aid to other countries that become customers of the arms producers.

One technique widely practiced, at least in the United States, is to cultivate the support of admirals and generals with the prospect of lucrative positions and directorships upon their retirement from active duty. It also helps the corporations if they can obtain appointments of their people to high level civilian positions in the nation's defense establishment. President Dwight D. Eisenhower expressed concern about what he called the "military-industrial complex" in his farewell address.

Other seriously harmful "external" costs imposed by various large corporations on people around the world include air and water pollution, contamination of food with persistent pesticides, fostering of drug-resistant bacteria by overuse of antibiotics on healthy livestock, recklessly injecting hormones into dairy cows, and experimenting on the public by promoting genetically modified foods before determining that they are safe. Other related issues involve laxity in food handling and inspection, undisclosed irradiation of food, and use of "low-level" radioactive materials in products sold to and/or used by the public.

Air pollution has made the natural problems of allergies much worse. Dr. Linda Ford, past president of the American Lung Association and current president of the Asthma and Allergy Center in Nebraska, says: "Air pollution definitely makes people with allergies more sensitive. Even in nonallergic people, diesel exhaust and ground-level ozone causes inflammation of air passages." (Quoted in "How Global Warming Affects Your Allergies" by Heidi Ridgley in the April/May 2002 issue of *National Wildlife*—see www.nwf.org/climate.)

These widespread effects would explain why some 35 million people in the United States now suffer from seasonal allergies (according to the American Academy of Allergy, Asthma and Immunology) as compared to the experience of Dr. John Bostick who first identified hay fever in 1819 after spending nine years just to find 28 cases, according to Dr. Ford, quoted in the same article.

Another even more serious disease that undoubtedly has been greatly aggravated by pollution is cancer. Statistical proof is difficult, if not impossible, because only a few generations ago the means for identifying cancer were lacking and most deaths were attributed vaguely to "old age" or "natural causes." There have been instances, however, where cause and effect are quite clear, such as Love Canal. Other areas in the vicinity of polluting industries have been found to have much higher rates of cancer (and other diseases) than the average for the population.

Corporations responsible for such lethal "externalities" attempt to escape responsibility by at least two strategies: (1) they demand absolute proof that the harmful effects are due to their operation rather than other sources, and (2) they counter proposed regulation by trumpeting exaggerated estimates of the cost and asserting that it would be passed on to consumers.

They and their allies use financial and political power to thwart government clean-up efforts and to influence academic research. They have succeeded in getting cancer-fighting organizations to limit their work to assisting victims and recommending healthy diets instead of investigating industrial causes of cancer.

Under corporate pressure, governments tend to put the burden on the general public rather than big business (Example: passenger automobiles in the US are required to meet strict emissions tests, while trucks, busses, and industry-favored sports utility vehicles (SUVs) are largely exempt—and factory smokestacks get delay after delay in pollution reduction.)

In many ways, capitalist enterprises use resources efficiently, to give them their due, and create wealth that can be used for education and for control and mitigation of pollution. Perhaps it was because they had no great wealth that industrial Communist societies permitted so much of their pollution to go untreated, and lack of wealth today means that developing countries need assistance to reduce pollution.

Some people say that if we put the necessary democratic and environmental constraints on market economics, then we will have abolished capitalism. Others favor a reformed capitalism that sustains democratic values rather than restrains them and a capitalism that includes all the costs to the environment—rather than an abolished capitalism. Such reform would include giving workers a legitimate right to bargain with corporations, breaking up powerful trusts, holding corporate officers criminally responsible for corporate crimes, and making it illegal for corporations to participate in any political process.

Perhaps capitalism is the only socio-economic system in world history that can function well in democracies. It causes democracy, because it brings into being a considerable middle class. This is a thesis in the book of Robert Heilbronner, *Twenty-first Century Capitalism* (1992).

The relationship between democracy and capitalism (market system) is a complex one. Big corporations misuse their powers, but small and middle sized companies (and entrepreneurs) give opportunities to individuals.

In the U.S. (and some other countries that have followed its example) there was what academics in political science and economics called a "mixed system" in which private businesses, producer cooperatives, consumer cooperatives, and government agencies all played their part. Then the "Chicago School" disciples of Milton Friedman largely prevailed in the US (and in Margaret Thatcher's Britain) with a new political and economic faith so opposed to any government activity or regulation that it could properly be described as "anarchy."

Many of us feel that small businesses competing by Adam Smith rules are fine, and if they so please their customers that they grow large, so be it. What is wrong is when businesses combine to stifle competition and improperly influence government. Corporations are NOT persons, and much harm was done by the US Supreme Court in a series of decisions that gave them even more rights than individuals. Limited liability without responsibility has caused much of the trouble we see today.

By 2000, according to a study by the Institute for Policy Studies, "The Top 200 corporations' combined sales were bigger than the combined economies of all countries minus the biggest 10....Between 1983 and 1999, the profits of the Top 200 firms grew 362.4 percent, while the number of people they employ grew by only 14.4 percent....U.S. corporations dominate the Top 200, with 82 slots (41 percent of the total). Japanese firms are second, with only 41 slots." (view in PDF at http://www.ips-dc.org/top200.htm)

The following proposals were submitted to the forum members as a summary of those on which all were thought to agree:

1. Corporations, especially the multinationals (also called transnationals), must be brought under control. They have extended their size and power to the point that they are a threat to the planet and its inhabitants. Some corporations are actually bigger than many national governments in the world. They are able to get free of environmental regulation by threatening governments that they will move to a more permissive jurisdiction. They undermine and destroy labor unions by similar threats or actual movement of factories to areas of low or nonexistent standards for wages, health, and safety.

2. Remove the legal fiction that a corporation is a person. Given that there are important differences between corporations and real people, corporations should not be awarded the rights of free speech and political activity that properly belong to citizens.

3. Improper influence on government officials must be prevented. Outright bribery is used in some countries. Elsewhere, large corporations and their wealthy controlling stockholders influence public officials by campaign contributions and by favors such as expense-paid trips to luxury resorts, interest-free loans, and free use of corporate jet planes. They also underwrite propaganda campaigns to help political parties and candidates. To circumvent election laws in the US they stop short of saying "vote for X" or "vote against Y" but come as close to that as possible. Although it is illegal for corporations to contribute to political campaigns, they seem to have done so by various loopholes and subterfuges.

4. Newspapers and broadcasters need to be freed from the control of corporate cartels. Since the Telecommunications Act of 1996 there has been a parade of media mergers and over 4,000 radio stations have been bought up in the United States, while television networks are now in the hands of huge corporations like General Electric, Viacom,

Disney, and Rupert Murdoch's News Corporation. Murdoch also controls large portions of the television and newspaper media in Great Britain, Australia, and elsewhere. Corporate media have done their best to hide corporate scandals and to downplay or distort any protests against corporations.

5. Corporate efforts to undermine pure food laws, to raise livestock under factory conditions with dangerous use of antibiotics and hormones, to treat food with hazardous radiation, to modify crops genetically without adequate testing, to patent life forms and traditional remedies, and to promote "killer" seeds that make farmers forever dependent on corporate suppliers, must be brought under control. This should be done by national laws to the extent possible and by new international controls under the UN or similar body.

6. Agencies of the United Nations need to be prevented from operating in secrecy in behalf of multinational corporations. On the world scene, global corporations (including global bankers and financial companies) dominate international agencies unrestrained by democratic safeguards. At the World Bank, IMF, and WTO the walls of secrecy should be removed, independent outside experts should be used, and the policy-makers and advisory groups should include balanced representation of the interests involved, not dominated by the global corporations. The World Bank should include experts not beholden to the financial community; e.g., economists from labor organizations, consumer groups, and the academic world, as well as environmental organizations and experts from the countries involved in their development programs, and the same should apply to the IMF. The WTO should include balanced representation of consumers as well as producers, and judges on its tribunals should be independent scientific experts who can distinguish legitimate environmental concerns from mere pretexts, especially in the matter of food safety.

7. Voting in the World Bank and IMF needs to be more democratic, instead of being based on financial investment that favors rich nations, especially the United States. Reform of the IMF must include keeping it out of politics. The enormous leverage of the IMF over democratic institutions in borrowing countries was made plain in South Korea's presidential elections, as the Fund insisted that all presidential candidates endorse the IMF bailout agreement.

8. Every available influence should be brought to bear by the UN, World Bank, IMF, etc., to prevent multinational corporations (in league with repressive governments) from driving local inhabitants off their land by pollution from poisons such as cyanide used in mining, by oil spills into water supplies, and by using violence against those who protest. There have been many instances, including Shell in Nigeria, BHP (Australia's largest company) in Papua New Guinea, Gemala Industries of Indonesia in occupied East Timor, DuPont in Goa, mining companies in the Philippines, and many others.

9. Regional trade agreements such as NAFTA and global agreements such as GATT should not be ratified without enforceable protections of the environment and workers rights. Prime examples of this need are the corporations that set up polluting factories in Mexico near the US border and get away with firing any employee who joins a union. Often police and armed forces of the host nation are used to coerce employees.

10. Steps should be taken by national and international authorities to stop the bidding war in which corporations extract subsidies, tax abatements, and exemption from environmental and human rights requirements in a competition among localities for the placement of corporate activities.

11. The "revolving door" for individuals who shuttle back and forth between government positions and corporate lobbying needs to be abolished. In the US former government administrators and congress-

men become lobbyists and many make as much as a million dollars annually. Some, like Henry Kissinger, form consulting firms that lobby without disclosing the names of corporations for whom they work.

12. Corporations should be prohibited from financing front organizations such as "think tanks" and purported grassroots organizations to advocate corporate interests, or at least their role should be publicly revealed.

13. Corporations should not be allowed to sponsor US presidential debates as Anheuser-Busch, U.S. Airways and 3Com did in 2000. After the original organizer, the League of Women Voters opened the debates to a third party candidate in 1980, the two major parties set up a Commission on Presidential Debates (run out of a political consulting firm's office in Washington, D.C.) that has set rules effectively excluding third party candidates.

14. People should be provided information on how to organize to deal with local issues—how to deal with Wal-Mart moving into a small town, or a corporate polluter nearby, cleaning up a polluted neighborhood, or how to oppose large developments that destroy a community's lifestyle. (Al Norman of "Sprawl-Busters" who has helped 88 smaller firms fight Wal-Mart, is one source.)

15. People who wish to do so should be encouraged to develop and put into practice local economies, beginning with local food economies, to shorten the distance between producers and consumers, to make the connections between the two more direct, and to make this local economic activity a benefit to the local community.

Other proposals supported by many or most forum members:

16. There should be a democratically chosen body on a global level to act as an umpire to enforce rules of the economic game.

17. Restore the "mixed system" in which private businesses, producer cooperatives, consumer cooperatives, and government agencies all played their part. This has largely been destroyed in the US and other countries where it used to flourish. Preserve it wherever it survives.

18. Corporations should be prohibited from donating to political parties or campaigns.

19. Political campaigns should be publicly financed to replace bribery by means of campaign finance.

20. Lobbying should be strictly limited by forbidding anything of value being offered to public officials.

21. Make corporate officers personally responsible for violating laws.

22. Make corporations report to the public, as well as shareholders, on their undertakings and plans that affect workers, consumers, and the environment.

23. In regard to the terms and length of copyrights on "intellectual property" the right balance needs to be achieved to provide inducement for creative work without locking it out of the public domain for an unreasonably long period. The same applies to patented inventions. In the US entertainment companies like Disney were successful in lobbying to extend the duration of copyright far beyond the lifetimes of the creators.

24. There should be a body such as the "Environmental Council" proposed by Earth Action to make binding decisions to protect the planet, perhaps by transforming an already existing UN institution, with its actions subject to approval by the General Assembly, combined with an expanded environmental role for the World Court.

25. All nations need to agree to implement simultaneously a range of measures to re-regulate global markets and corporations in order to

restore genuine democracy, environmental protection, and peace around the world. This is because no nation or group of nations alone can control global capital nor implement vital economic, social or environmental policies that might incur market or corporate displeasure. A method for breaking this impasse is proposed by the International Simultaneous Policy Organization (ISPO), whose website is www.simpol.org.

26. If there is no other way to overcome the favored status US courts have given to corporations, it would have to be accomplished by constitutional amendment, making the limitations and responsibilities of corporations so clear the courts could not interpret them away.

27. Corporations should be required to have national charters rather than seeking charters in more permissive internal or external jurisdictions.

28. Foreign corporations should be subject to the same taxes and laws as domestic corporations.

29. Since the historical basis of all corporate charters is service beneficial to the general public, any corporate activity not beneficial to the public, especially if it involves explicitly illegal actions, should be cause for charter revocation both in the case of the parent corporation and of its foreign subsidiaries.

30. National laws protecting the environment, public health, safety, and human rights within any country should also apply to its corporations and their subsidiaries when operating outside that country.

31. Public officials should be prevented from holding secret meetings with heads of corporations and financial institutions, as at the Council on Foreign Relations, the Bilderberg, and the Trilateral Commission.

32. Businesses should be encouraged to use energy and resources efficiently without paying subsidies. In the efficient energy use chapter of

Jim Bell's book he cites numerous large corporation who have invested in energy and resource use efficiency measures "and in every case their return on investment was better than their investments in their product lines."

33. As proposed by Jim Bell, governments should use experts from economics and accounting to determine the true cost of various goods, and then pass laws to include externalities, such as environmental damage, normally neglected in retail prices. Possible questions: Does this method create a huge bureaucracy of accountants to figure the true costs and lawyers to dispute them? Who gets the price increase? Does it become excess profit for the corporations? Does the government tax it away and use the proceeds to offset pollution and hazardous waste? If so, how do we prevent it being frittered away in litigation as is being done regarding the SuperFund taxes that were supposed to clean up toxic waste? What about the effect of these higher prices on GDP? National production is conventionally measured by market prices, so wouldn't the damage to environment and humans now be counted as an increase in GDP?

34. The obverse of true cost pricing is "The Neuman Proposal," which would have the government pay individuals to reduce their travel by car or plane in order to decrease emission of greenhouse gasses that contribute to global climate change. This raises questions of the possibility of enactment, the accuracy and administrative cost of determining these subsidies, and the possibility of fraud or misuse.

35. Limit the size that corporations can attain or their ability to merge to reduce competition. Of the world's 100 largest economic entities, 51 are now corporations and 49 are countries according to the Institute for Policy Studies. The world's top 200 corporations account for over a quarter of economic activity on the globe while employing less than one percent of its workforce. http://www.ips-dc.org/top200.htm

36. Remove the "limited liability" of corporations (Inc., LLC, Ltd., SA, NV, GmbH), making the liability of corporations real and full, so it will have an impact on the shareholders and will guide them to more responsible actions. Limited liability without responsibility has caused much of the trouble we see today.

37. Some people propose that capitalism be abolished. Richard Moore opined, "that if we put the necessary democratic and environmental constraints on market economics, then we will have abolished capitalism." Others would go further to replace markets and private investment entirely.

38. Localized economic control should replace multinational corporate control. If there is local economic control, then democracy may continue as a healthy form of government. Locally elected leaders may come together as the democratic representatives in a confederation.

39. There should be a large international peace-keeping force under the control of the U.N. or some other agency that ensures equitable distribution of natural resources and peace, after all weapons of mass destruction have been destroyed.

40. Large numbers of people should reduce using energy sufficiently to let the power brokers know who really is in control.

41. People could stop eating beef. Just in Central America alone 35 million people are now either landless or own too little land to support themselves while the transnational corporations have continued to drive the locals away and clear forest to raise beef cattle (1992 figures).

4

Making Monetary Systems Work to Benefit People

This chapter asserts that control of the world's finances by major banks and corporations, in league with the International Monetary Fund, must be broken. The IMF acts to protect banks and speculators from losses due to bad judgment, while pressuring borrowing governments to take actions that favor penetration by multinational corporations and curtailment of government protections for its citizens. Also considered are concentration of financial power, mismeasurement of GDP, and the merits of local currencies.

There is an old saying that "money makes the world go round." It reflects the extent to which control of money determines so much else that happens on this planet. Presidents of the United States like to be described as "the leader of the free world." Other holders of public office throughout the world likewise consider themselves "in control." In reality they often are merely responding to the pressures and carrying out the wishes of those who control the money.

Wealth is known to be quite concentrated, although recent global figures are hard to find, especially for wealth rather than income. According to a recent study by World Bank economist Branko Milanovic, about 50 million people who made up the top one percent in the world's five billion population had 9.5% of the world's income in 1993. That was more than the whole bottom half who had only 8.5% (published January 18, 2002, in the *Economic Journal*).

The contrast among nations is shown by figures compiled in 1992 by the United Nations Development Program (UNDP). They found that the 20% of the world's people who live in the world's wealthiest countries received 82.7% of the world's income, while only 1.4% of the world's income went to the 20% who live in the world's poorest countries.

In the United States, headquarters of many of the multinational corporations, the top 5% of U.S. families received 20.3% of total money income in 1996, and the top fifth, 46.8%, while only 4.2% went to the bottom fifth. As for wealth, Federal Reserve figures for 1989 showed that the richest 1% of American households accounted for nearly 40% of the nation's wealth, and the top 20% accounted for 80% of the wealth.

Wherever figures are available, wealth turns out to be even more unevenly divided than income, but figures are hard to get because the wealthy prefer not to disclose that information. Not only wealth is concentrated, but also power.

Such banking families as Rothschild, Morgan, and Rockefeller have long exerted a powerful influence on public policy, including the financing of wars. In modern times, control is largely exercised by major financial houses and huge corporations whose interests are promoted by the International Monetary Fund (IMF), the World Bank, agencies for export financing, and regional development organizations.

There is much confusion about the functions of the IMF and the World Bank. Both were created at the Bretton Woods Conference in 1944 during World War II. The original and official name of the World Bank is the International Bank for Reconstruction and Development, which is a better description of its purpose. Instead of being a bank in the usual sense, it was intended to provide financial aid by making and insuring loans where needed to promote economic recovery throughout the world. Ostensibly, it is still pursuing that objective, but its methods have been criticized as counterproductive and its management has acknowledged that reform is needed.

The IMF's original function, on the other hand, was to maintain fixed and stable exchange rates among the currencies of member nations. This was largely based on a standing offer of the United States to other governments that it would buy or sell gold at a fixed price of $35 per ounce from its huge hoard at Fort Knox. When that policy was dropped and national currencies were allowed to "float" in the 1970s, the IMF found a new mission. It began to offer loans to developing countries with strings attached, and later added guarantees of loans by international private banks with similar conditions attached.

When a currency crisis occurs now, as it did in Asia late in 1997 and in Argentina in 2002, for example, the IMF remedy is to demand austerity and deregulation in exchange for additional loans or loan extensions. Its policies are thus in step with those of the World Bank for "structural adjustment" that have caused such opportunities for big business and disasters for local populations as described in Chapter 3.

In the Asian crisis, for example, the global financial powers hastily put together a rescue package, bailing out the unwise investments of banks and others. South Korea, one of the major recipients of funding, did not punish corrupt politicians involved in the crisis, but agreed to give foreign corporations more access to its domestic market, open its bond market, and speed up the opening of branch offices by foreign banks and stock companies. In addition the IMF arrogantly insisted that all candidates in South Korea's presidential elections endorse the IMF bailout agreement.

Another method of dealing with currency crises has been propping up of national currencies by foreign exchange operations of governments or their central banks at the expense of the public. Experience has shown that such efforts have only temporary effects at great cost. An example was the vain and costly effort in 1992 by central banks in England and Germany to support a weak British pound. This was the time George Soros' hedge fund won an estimate $1 billion profit betting the banks would not succeed. The British pound fell 41% in eleven months, as measured against the Japanese yen, and Britain had to withdraw from the Exchange Rate Mechanism (ERM) for stabilizing European currencies. On another occasion, more than $50 billion of US taxpayers' money was used to bolster the Mexican peso at the end of 1994, mainly benefiting Wall Street financial interests.

One answer to the crises caused by such speculation in currencies could be the tax proposed by the late Nobel-Prize-winning Yale economist James Tobin that would discourage currency speculation by making it less profitable. His proposal is promoted by Attac, a 27,000-member organization in France, the Association for the Taxation of Financial Transactions for the Aid of Citizens. The Tobin tax at one-quarter percent would raise about $250 billion a year, exceeding five times all current international aid, but could not be levied by any single country without causing financial companies to move to more permissive venues.

Another proposal to stabilize exchange rates would be to base currencies on actual commodities rather than existing credit money that is subject to risk by the herd mentality that drives speculators.

Money has come almost exclusively under the control of privately owned banks. The history of money runs from barter without money, to commodities used to define the value of other goods, and to rare items such as gold and silver generally accepted as payment for other goods and services. Then governments started making coins of gold and silver as a convenient means of insuring purity and accurate weight.

The next development was for goldsmiths in the Middle Ages to accept gold for safekeeping, issuing paper documents as receipts, which were found to be more convenient to carry than the actual metal. This led to the discovery by goldsmiths that these receipts, which were in effect paper money, remained in circulation for considerable times before being used to claim the precious metal, and so they issued receipts for more gold than they actually had.

These receipts were issued to borrowers who were expected to repay the amount with interest. Loaning at interest being forbidden by the

Christian church at that time, this banking operation became an attractive trade for Jews.

Meanwhile, governments began to issue paper money that promised redemption in precious metals, usually gold. They also, in time, discovered they could get away with issuing more paper than they had gold reserves to back up. Most, perhaps all, currency throughout the world is now redeemable only for more paper, and its purchasing power depends wholly on public confidence.

Banks also discovered that they could create money in another form by simply crediting a customer's account with a balance equal to the amount of a loan document signed by the customer. Just as goldsmith's receipts were not all claimed at once, the balances in customers' bank accounts are not all claimed at once. Thus the banks are able to issue such credits amounting to many times the bank's capital, the ratio being set by bank regulators.

With the purchasing power of currency depending entirely on public confidence (and the herd mentality of Wall Street), it is apparent that the structure is extremely fragile. If the public fears run-away inflation, a run on banks is likely. To build confidence and to ensure that banks' profits from interest are not eroded over time, central banks take deflationary measures whenever there is a hint of inflation and regardless of the calamitous rise in unemployment that often occurs.

As another way of maintaining public confidence, central banks also call on the government to bail out (with public funds) financial firms deemed "too big to fail." This allows bankers to take bigger risks, with profits going to the bankers while debts and bank failures are at the expense of the public.

The important interest rate decisions are made outside the structures of government that are answerable to the public. In the United States, whose dollars have become the *de facto* medium for international exchange, the Federal Reserve Board sits atop a banking hierarchy. Its members are insulated from government by long overlapping term appointments and control the 12 regional Federal Reserve Banks that actually issue the U.S. currency and whose shares are owned by other banks. FRB Chairman Alan Greenspan, first appointed by President Reagan, has become possibly the most powerful influence on the world economy.

The results of monetary policy exercised by the central banks to counter business cycles are usually judged by the rate of inflation, imperfectly measured, and by economic growth, measured very imperfectly by Gross Domestic Product (GDP). As noted in Chapter 1, that measure is seriously flawed.

For example, when a mother pays for child care, transportation, and outside meals, so she can work for wages, both her wages and expenses are counted in GDP, but her previous work in the home was not counted. Also, environmentally destructive activities are counted in GDP, as are the costs of repairing or counteracting the destruction.

For more detail, see *Beyond Globalization* by Hazel Henderson (Kumarian Press, 1999), chapter 2, and *Playing with the Numbers* by Richard A. Stimson (Westchester Press, 1999), chapter 3 (www.stimson.homestead.com).

The Bank of England and the new European Central Bank now have similar autonomy and the same "neo-liberal" economic philosophy as the FRB, the World Bank, and the IMF. The result is the policy of "scarce money" and people who are willing to work remain unemployed because potential customers for the goods they would produce lack the money to buy them, and businesses will not hire workers if there is no market for the products.

Economist Stuart Chase explained this in 1934 during the Great Depression when millions wanted to work and could not find jobs, the rich were hoarding money or buying property at distress prices, mortgages were being foreclosed, and there were runs on banks:

"The ten million unemployed in this country...would gladly take a volume of goods which would make factory wheels hum. The factory wheels are silent because the unemployed have no money." Chase went on to observe that production could keep on rolling if somehow people could be provided with cash. But that is "inflation" if people are equipped with money outside the "rules of the game." Those rules require that private bankers control the supply of money, manufacturing it by issuing business loans and crediting checking accounts.

"Private bankers cry to high heaven," Chase noted, "when the government proposes to create some money of its own against, let us say, public works. Why is this more reprehensible than creating money against a shoddily built apartment house which may never be rented?"

During that Great Depression another form of money was invented by municipalities when their tax receipts were insufficient to pay teachers, police, firemen, and other employees. Instead of legal tender they printed other pieces of paper called "scrip," that the cities would accept for tax payment and many local merchants agreed to accept. This expedient allowed many city workers to remain employed and merchants to pay their property taxes and to trade with each other. Although scrip became very successful in some places, the banks got it abolished as soon as they could.

Similar arrangements have been created among buyers and sellers without the use of government-created currency or bank-created credit. They were especially useful to decrease unemployment and business failures during the 1980s recession. Computer software is now available that enables people to break the type of impasse described by Stuart Chase.

One of the best known of "community currency" systems is the rapidly spreading "usury-free" LETS [Local Employment Trading System—sometimes called Local Exchange Trading System] of Michael Linton who lived in the Comox Valley on Vancouver Island in British Columbia, Canada, where many people were unemployed due to a money shortage. They trade their goods and services for those of others in the system, thus creating their own money. (www.cyberclass.net)

The LETS system is based on a "mutual credit" system proposed by Silvo Gesell in the early 1900s. While these systems remain clearly local, there are proposals to turn them into national systems such as that proposed by J. Walter Plinge (http://ebean390.tripod.com/drwalt.htm).

Other community currencies have also been developed, for which the "Ithaca Hours," established at Ithaca, New York (www.lightlink.com/hours/ithacahours), has become the model. This differs from mutual credit systems as it is a pure fiat currency. The RGT currency, similar to Ithaca Hours, afforded extensive bypassing of official currency during the recent crisis in Argentina. Similar systems exist in Brazil, Uruguay, Chile, and Spain (www.cyberclass.net/argentina.htm).

While many community currencies fail to provide for long-term borrowing, the long-established Swiss WIR (Wirtschaftsring-Genossenschaft—German for economic cooperative) and Swedish JAK (Jord, Arbete, Kapital—Swedish for land, labor, capital) systems are said to have resolved this problem.

JAK began as a cooperative savings and loan association in 1965 and was granted official bank status by the Swedish government in 1997, resulting in members' savings being covered by deposit guarantees. According to its official web site, it has over 21,000 members served by 80 trained volunteers in an interest-free banking system, whose main purpose is to provide interest-free loans to members. They also are able to earmark their savings for designated local enterprises. JAK has a commitment to "spreading information about the ill effects of the prevailing interest-bearing monetary system." (www.jak.se— in English)

WIR, under the Swiss federal banking law since 1936, and known as WIR Bank since 1998, grew out of an economic cooperative founded in 1934 as a result of the Great Depression. It attempted to relieve the money shortage, or liquidity crisis, by applying the concept of "interest-free money" from liberal economic theory, which was opposed to charging interest and led to the concept that idle money should depreciate. At that time of crisis, according to the history given on the WIR web site (www.wir.ch), associations were formed in the United States, Europe, and throughout the world, for the exchange of goods (barter) among members, and WIR was patterned on a Nordic model.

When the Depression was over, other such cooperatives disappeared. WIR continued, but the ideal of interest-free money was abandoned and modest interest charged for WIR loans and paid on participations in the cooperative. However, holdings in WIR money still do not bear interest. The idea of charging a tax on idle money was never actually applied. The principle of mutual aid among participants remains a priority.

In 1992-98 WIR Bank revised its capital structure, entered commercial activity in new market segments, began global financing of building construction in combined accounts of WIR credits and Swiss francs. In 2000 it offered services to the general public in Swiss francs. (www.wir.ch— French, German, and Italian versions).

In addition to community currencies are proposals for commodity-backed currencies for the purpose of resolving inequities in foreign currency exchanges. Early proposals came from Walter Bagehot in 1872 and later from Ralph Borsodi and J. M. Keynes in the early 1900s. Modern examples include the Terra of Bernard Lietaer, a former senior executive of the central bank of Belgium, expressed as a specified basket of raw materials, and a proposal made by J. W. Smith.

Entrepreneurs seeking to start or expand a business can get financing from banks or issuance of corporate bonds only with the promise of paying interest. The alternative seems to be to offer equity, or a share of the profits, rather than interest payments, as is said to be allowed in Islamic banking where interest or "usury" is forbidden by religion (as it once was in Christianity).

Unless systems such as those described above can grow rapidly to replace conventional banking and fiat money, there still remains the need to reform the national and international systems that dominate the world economy. For a comprehensive overview of alternate money systems, see Strohalm's Links to Economic Change (http://www.strohalm.nl/bookmarks/alles.htm).

The following proposals were submitted to the forum members as a summary of those on which all were thought to agree:

1. Control of the world's finances by major banks and corporations, in league with the International Monetary Fund, must be broken. The IMF acts to protect banks and speculators from losses due to bad judgment, while pressuring borrowing governments to take actions that favor penetration by multinational corporations and curtailment of government protections for its citizens.

2. Any international organizations such as IMF, the World Bank, and various regional development agencies that make grants or loans to assist nations in financial crises should not be under the exclusive control of bankers; they should be responsible and accountable to elected representatives of the world's people. The agents of major banks and corporations tend to do what is in their own interest rather than that of the affected populations.

3. No such organizations should be allowed to operate in secret, and they should be required to consult with non-governmental organizations; otherwise, conditions imposed on recipients may have onerous consequences that are unknown to the public until too late.

4. These international organizations must not require any nation, as a condition of aid, to curtail any services or protections it affords its people, or to sell off any government operations to private companies. There have been past instances when well-run government operations were forcibly privatized with resulting price increases, loss of employment and/or damage to the environment.

5. Nor should these agencies require recipients to charge fees for children to attend school and for people to access basic health services. User fees for education discourage school attendance and user fees for health services lead to preventable death and disease.

6. These international organizations must also not require actions that favor penetration by multinational corporations in preference to local economic activity. Such actions have often deprived inhabitants of their traditional use of land and forced them to seek a living in the cities after they were driven off their land by armed forces or by poisoning of their streams with industrial waste, such as cyanide used in gold mining.

7. The "neo-liberal" economic approach that permeates these agencies must be overcome; the attitude of their bankers and multinational corporate allies places greater importance on rights of banks and corporations than on the liberties and economic welfare of the population.

8. Competition must be restored to the financial world by breaking the grip of monopolistic chains of banks, stockbrokers, and insurance companies that have crowded out independent entities and formed dangerous financial corporations across national and functional boundaries. In recent years these chains have grown, not mainly by providing better service to customers, but through mergers and acquisitions contrary to the intent of antitrust laws in various nations. The US Congress, after receiving many favors and contributions from financial firms, repealed the Glass-Steagall Act of 1933 and allowed banks again to sell financial securities and insurance.

9. Local mediums of exchange should be encouraged to reduce dependence on national currencies, international bankers, and manipulated exchange rates. Scrip not issued by governments or banks has been successfully introduced in some localities, including LETS (Local Employment/Exchange Trading System).

10. Likewise, mutual credit and barter in situations where appropriate should weaken the grip of the dominant financial institutions. New information technologies are making these arrangements more feasible.

11. Production should be measured without the errors of present Gross Domestic Product (GDP) calculations, which among other things, ignore value produced outside the money economy, such as work in the home, and count the destruction of natural resources as production.

12. Governments and non-governmental organizations should encourage employee ownership of businesses, thus guarding against short-sighted policies of absentee ownership. Banks must not be allowed to dictate the selection of management, as is often the case at present.

Other proposals supported by many or most forum members:

13. Nations that owe crushing debt because of past international banking policies need relief from that debt. International efforts should be made to recover funds diverted from those countries by leaders who embezzled them, and new grants or loans should be offered only when conditions are met to safeguard them from misuse. A bank that lends, without precautions, to a military dictator who then absconds with the money leaving his citizenry holding the debt is a predatory lender. International predatory lending laws could absolve poor citizens from repayment of such debt.

14. Private banks and bankers, necessarily having a vested interest in monetary decisions, must not be in control of central banks; and they must not be allowed to cause widespread unemployment by raising interest rates on the pretext of inflation risk.

15. Banks and money systems are the public's economic infrastructure like roads, rivers, and airspace. Bankers should be trustees with a fiduciary duty to be devoid of self-interest and to operate banks for the sole benefit of the communities and nations in which they operate. Banks should never be run for private profit, and no country should permit foreign nationals to own their banks. As a fiduciary operation, no bank

should be allowed to engage in speculation in currency or other instruments.

16. National currencies must not be propped up by foreign exchange operations of governments or their central banks at the expense of the public. Experience has shown that such efforts have only temporary effects at great cost.

17. Instead of financing government services by taxes that are mostly imposed on productive activity, funds should be obtained by taxes and/or fees on externalized costs (pollution, health hazards, environmental damage, etc.) and financial transactions (via the Tobin tax). To prevent corporations from escaping taxation these charges should be imposed at the global level, partly financing worldwide needs and partly apportioned to member states. The benefits would be relief of existing taxes on useful work, discouragement of operations harmful to humans and the environment, and limitation of speculation in currencies and financial instruments that amounts to gambling and disrupts normal commerce.

18. The development of currencies—local, national, or worldwide—based on actual commodities rather than existing fiat money should be encouraged, along with mutual credit systems.

19. Support and encourage the restoration of a "mixed system" in which private businesses, producer cooperatives, consumer cooperatives, and government agencies all played their part prior to the ascendancy of the "Chicago School" disciples of Milton Friedman.

5

Democratizing the Communications Media

✦

(based on a summary by Liane Casten in Chicago with Richard Stimson)

Concentrated ownership and control is dangerous enough in other areas, but it is especially harmful with regard to communications media. That is because it allows a few powerful people to limit and distort what information other people receive.

In 1999, when there were still some restrictions media moguls were trying to break down, Rupert Murdoch and his Australian company, News Corporation, controlled over 70% of the press in Australia, and over 35% in Britain. They also had the New York *Post*, the *Village Voice*, *New York* magazine, the Boston *Herald*, the Chicago *Sun-Times*, the Twentieth Century Fox film studio, and Metromedia television stations in the United States, as well as satellite television in much of the world.

Time-Warner and Bertelsmann AG were then making major acquisitions, and the three traditional US television networks (before Murdoch's Fox) were in the hands of General Electric, Westinghouse, and the Disney Corporation.

By 2002 the monopolistic tendency had gone much further and information was increasingly dominated by entertainment. Viacom, owner of Paramount motion picture studios, book publishers, MTV and other cable channels, replaced Westinghouse as owner of the CBS television network. A special issue of *The Nation* (January 7-14, 2002) contained a color chart summarizing the holdings of the "Big Ten" corporations that make up the media cartel.

These media-controlling corporations were shown to have revenues ranging from AT&T's $555 billion and General Electric's $130 billion down to Bertelsmann's $17 billion and News Corporation's $12 billion. The chart showed many joint ventures and percentage shares of ownership involving various of the ten companies.

Since, at least in the United States, polls have shown that most people rely on television for their news, that medium has special importance. The Big Ten generally include both the studios that produce content with the channels that disseminate it. Al Franken, one of several people "The Nation" asked to comment on the chart, explained how this happened.

"In 1995 the networks prevailed after years of fierce lobbying before Congress" in having the financial interest and syndication rules (fin-syn) rescinded that had prevented networks from owning more than a certain percentage of the shows they aired. Now, he wrote, "The same people who are scheduling the shows are making the shows, so what you see reflects the tastes of fewer and fewer people."

The principle that content and distribution should be kept independent of each other is also breached with regard to DVDs (digital video discs). CSS (Content Scrambling System) prevents copying of DVDs and any software used for playing back DVDs must pay the major studios for a license. The world is split into six regions with DVD discs and players that are incompatible with those in other regions. Similarly, the incompatibility of television systems (and camcorders) in different parts of the world serves commercial interests at the expense of public convenience.

A major political victory for the media oligarchy was the Telecommunications Reform Act of 1996. Overwhelmingly supported by both major parties, it effectively removed virtually all limits in the communications and entertainment industries. Congress also extended the duration of patents and copyrights, allowing firms like Disney to milk the profits from artistic work long after the originator is dead.

The industry's political power is phenomenal. According to the Center for Public Integrity the fifty largest media companies and four of their trade associations spent $111.3 million between 1996 and mid-2000 for Washington lobbying, not counting millions of dollars in campaign contributions.

All of the Big Ten in the chart have television holdings, including multiple channels and production facilities for content. General Electric, for example, has the NBC network and percentage shares in cable channels that include CNBC, MSNBC, A&E, History, Biography, AMC, Bravo, plus stakes in regional channels, Europe and Asia. Disney, with six production companies, 30 television stations, the ABC network, and Disney channels in over 140 countries, also has shares in a half-dozen other channels, plus theme parks in California, Florida, Paris, Tokyo, and Hong Kong.

AT&T, with 60 million US telephone customers and 5 million corporate clients worldwide, also distributes television programs in 175 countries, has shares in television channels in the US, Asia, Europe, Canada, and South America. It is the largest cable company pending a $47 billion sale to Comcast.

In the print media category, AOL/Time-Warner has more than 40 magazines and three book publishing companies, plus a stake in the Book-of-the-Month Club. It is the leading consumer magazine publisher in Britain. Bertelsmann, the biggest broadcaster and main film producer in Europe, has 11 daily newspapers in Germany and Eastern Europe, many magazines in Europe and the US, and is the largest book publishing conglomerate in the US with Knopf, Random House, Modern Library, and Doubleday.

The dominance of entertainment over information is illustrated by the film studios, libraries, and cinemas they own: Warner Bros. (AOL/Time-Warner), Viacom (Paramount and other studios plus cinema theaters in US, Canada, Europe, Asia, and South America), Disney, News Corporation (Twentieth Century Fox), SONY (Columbia Pictures, Screen Gems, Loew's Theaters), Vivendi Universal (Universal, world's second largest film library, and 3 cinema theater companies), and Liberty Media Corp. (spun off from AT&T, has shares in six movie companies).

Music distribution is also important to AOL/Time-Warner, Bertelsmann, SONY, Vivendi Universal, and Liberty Media. Many of the companies have theme parks and professional sports teams. Further interests range from General Electric's nuclear reactors and financial services, through Disney's cartoon merchandise, to Vivendi Universal's hundreds of recycling, landfill, and incinerator sites worldwide, plus 220 advertising agencies in 66 countries.

Internet involvement of the Big Ten includes Bertelmann's search engines, Internet service in Europe by Bertelmann and Vivendi Universal, AOL/Time-Warner's AOL and Compuserve Internet service, SONY's Internet service in Japan, and many websites related to their television channels.

Access to the Internet is overwhelmingly through computers running Microsoft's Windows operating system and its Explorer net browser. This virtual monopoly was achieved by methods ruled by US courts to be illegal restraint of trade under the antitrust laws. Unlike the open-source Linux system, Windows keeps its source code secret and Microsoft uses its market strength to get its way with computer manufacturers and software applications companies.

Media companies and other owners of "intellectual property" have not only extended the duration of copyrights but also used the patent laws beyond their original intention. Software patents that forbid copying the programmer's code are reasonable, but patents are being granted for the "method" of achieving a goal, even if different code is created. Software patents are often just elementary applications of mathematics or generic concepts.

Inventors have long understood that patent law did not allow patenting a device that any competent mechanic could create. Under corporate political pressure, patent grantors, at least in the U.S., seem to have forgotten the traditional limitations and accepted outrageous extensions (even to the extent of patenting living organisms and traditional native remedies).

Media problems have been discussed on the Blue Ear Forum, which consists mostly of journalists and writers around the world. A guest participant was Robert McChesney of the University of Illinois at Urbana-Champaign, author of "Rich Media, Poor Democracy" (University of Illinois Press, 1999), a book that dealt with many of the issues discussed in this chapter. Further information can be found at www.robertmcchesney.com.

In another book with co-author John Nichols, "It's the Media Stupid" (Seven Stories Press, 2000) they declared: "No, the media system is not the sole cause of our political crisis, nor even the primary cause, but it reinforces every factor contributing to the crisis, and it fosters a climate in which the implementation of innovative democratic solutions is rendered all but impossible."

When "The Nation" published its special issue with the chart showing the holdings of the Big Ten, discussion on Blue Ear heated up and Jay Rosen of Columbia University chided members for not differentiating between ownership and control, and for implying that control was so complete it was hopeless to oppose it. He asserted that freedom of expression of those in the forum belied their claims of media control.

After various members of that forum responded to Rosen questioning whether he had any concern about recent developments affecting the media, however, he admitted concern and declared:

"I'm worried about the rise of market values to a position where they trump all other values, such as public service, professionalism, truth, accuracy, genuine art, genuine popular culture, honesty, ethics. I think that dismantling the regulatory powers of the Federal government over broadcasting was a cave-in to major media corporations, and fully in line with the Republican party's agenda during those years, which was to evacuate any notion of the public interest beyond the 'verdict of the marketplace.'"

The tight control of the communications media by major corporations leaves a few cracks and crevices, as Rosen pointed out, where information can seep through, such as Internet forums, small circulation publications, letters to the editor, local access cable channels, and occasional documentaries on public television or even some commercial TV reports.

Overall, though, the information most people receive avoids issues about which the corporations owning the media (or their advertisers) are uncomfortable. Several examples will illustrate this point.

Very little has been revealed about dioxin as the U.S. Environmental Protection Agency (EPA) has kept the scientific results of dioxin reassessment bottled up under both Clinton and Bush. Miniscule amounts are extremely harmful to humans. One source of dioxin is the bleaching with chlorine of newsprint—not something the major newspapers want to talk about. Dioxin is a component of Agent Orange, whose connection with illnesses of Vietnam veterans was long covered up by government and media.

Another public health hazard that has been kept under wraps is the presence of bovine growth hormones (BGH) in milk and other dairy products in the U.S. They are causative for breast, prostate, and colon cancer, and diabetes according to studies in such peer-reviewed journals as "Lancet" and "Science." They are in school lunch programs in the United States but banned in Canada and the European Union. Political connections of Monsanto, the only maker of these hormones, may explain why the EPA and the Food and Drug Administration (FDA) have not acted. When two television reporters at a Fox station in Florida tried to report the dangers of BGH, they were fired.

One more of many possible examples is that much of the nuclear radiation continually leaching into water tables and communities is from polluted sites never cleaned up by General Electric. Since that company owns NBC, no disclosure can be expected there. Some of the major media have been unable to avoid mentioning the dioxin in the Hudson River that GE refuses to clean up.

In the political arena, U.S. television networks allowed a commission of the Republican and Democratic parties to exclude candidates of other parties from the presidential debates in 2000. In fact, the Green Party candidate, Ralph Nader, was forcibly excluded from the room.

There is a website completely devoted to media censorship, which can be found at www.projectcensored.org. Free emails about items under-covered in the press can be obtained by subscription and the media research group issues an annual list of under-covered over-covered news items. The director of Project Censored is Dr. Peter Phillips, Associate Professor of Sociology at Sonoma State University in California.

Media coverage of news can be influenced by considerations of patriotism, (not only in the United States). According to Phillips, "Marc Herold, an economics professor at the University of New Hampshire compiled a summation of the death toll in Afghanistan-saying that over 4,000 civilians died from U.S. bombs-more than died at the World Trade Center. Yet only a handful of newspapers covered his story."

Phillips also noted that both the BBC and the Times of India published reports several months before 9-11 that the U.S. was then planning an invasion of Afghanistan. The Unocal oil pipeline from the Caspian Sea region was to be built through Afghanistan and the U.S. needed a cooperative government in power. He cited report from France regarding how the Bush administration, shortly after assuming office, slowed down FBI investigations of al-Qaeda and terrorist networks in Afghanistan in order to deal with the Taliban on oil. These, and other suspicious matters including the millions of dollars made on pre-9-11 put options on United and American Airlines stocks, have largely been ignored by the mainstream US news media.

Liane Casten was appointed by Project Censored as one of the national judges to select the 12 most censored stories of the year 2001. After reviewing the 26 contenders, she wrote:

"Power corrupts; absolute power corrupts absolutely. When the media become the self-serving gatekeepers that lock out from public scrutiny reports of government and corporate corruption or criminality, then here is little left but the runaway consolidation and nearly complete corruption of media power. Thanks to FCC chair, Michael Powell, and the present administration, the grip— in process since the Telecommunication Act of 1996, has only become tighter. Blather, public relations and propaganda take the place of significant information, while a corporate agenda now insinuates itself into the classrooms— affecting ever younger and younger minds. Children are being trained for the marketplace, not the polling place. Critical thinking and vigorous debate are becoming unpatriotic.

"When we have media conglomerations now aligned with the power structure—in all their varied and myriad connections, (from regulators to profiteers) we have the perfect blanket that covers over the rapaciousness, the greed, and the immoral indifference to human life that constitutes any definition of evil. With no public scrutiny, both corporations and the government can go about their business of keeping the world safe for Silicon Valley's technologies, for McDonnell Douglas's newest killing machine, for Coca Cola's and Nike's third world labor policies and pay structures, or for Occidental Petroleum's pipeline to oil.

"And this true agenda is being carried out with greater arrogance and abandon because the mainstream media no longer report these crimes or hold the perpetrators accountable. Often the criminal perpetrators–like polluting Disney and GE—are the very corporations that own the media. The agenda is war (anywhere) and missile sales, not peace; profit now, not human health or a concern for the future of this planet.

"While the US. military is making the world safe for U.S. capitalism, and while it destroys everything in its wake in the process—from local resources to human lives, our own country and indeed the world continues to pay a devastating price. Whole generations in the U.S. and abroad are now suffering, are butchered, starved and manipulated into poverty and whole generations will continue to suffer and be manipulated by forces beyond their control, unreported and ignored by most media outlets. As Bob McChesney wisely stated, 'The corruption of the system would be difficult to exaggerate.'"

There is also a organization dedicated to "Fairness & Accuracy in Reporting" (FAIR), that has email notices and a website www.fair.org to expose incomplete and/or inaccurate information in the media.

Members of the FixGov forum seem to have arrived at the following consensus on necessary reforms for the media:

1. Information media (including newspapers, magazines, books, television, radio, digital communication, and cinema) must be free of government censorship of facts and opinions. What are reasonable restrictions involving national security and decency will always be debatable. Governments tend to err on the side of too much restriction.

2. The media must also be free of censorship by commercial cartels, which have been concentrating ownership of all types of media across national boundaries, putting these corporations in position to block and/or distort information to suit their commercial and political interests. As many people recognize what is happening, public trust in the media is undermined.

3. In the case of print media, full information and diversity of views is most likely to prevail when there is the maximum of competition. Government should not interfere with publication, but it should enforce strong antitrust laws to prevent economic power from driving out competition.

4. The broadcast media should likewise consist of independent television and radio stations, not having interlocking ownership and control with print media, and certainly not dominated by parent companies that are primarily interested in entertainment products and/or conflicting commercial activities.

5. Although the BBC has built a reputation for quality television and often broadcasts information displeasing to the government in power, it is dangerous, in general, for government to have a monopoly or dominance of the airwaves, as demonstrated in many countries where that situation has turned broadcasting into a government propaganda machine.

6. In the United States the Public Broadcasting System once provided a useful counterpoint to commercial television, but the attacks of Newt Gingrich on public television have largely converted it into an imitation of commercial TV with sponsored messages and promotional announcements. National Public Radio has retained more of its objectivity under this pressure.

7. Government does have an important role in broadcasting, however, because frequencies have been allocated under international agreement and the spectrum available in each country is controlled by government, unlike the unlimited possibilities for print media in a free society. Broadcast rights should be auctioned periodically for the highest bid offered by a responsible party guaranteeing to provide a public service in an equitable manner.

8. During election campaigns, in particular, broadcasters should be required to provide a reasonable amount of free time for political discussions with all candidates treated equally. There should also by something along the lines of the "Fairness Doctrine" formerly enforced by the United States Federal Communications Commission to require that if one point of view is presented on the air equal time must be given to opposing opinions.

9. A limit on commercial messages (including their own promotions) should be a condition of broadcast licenses, as it was until the 1980s in the United States, and certainly 100% commercial programs known as "infomercials" should be completely prohibited.

10. Newspapers and broadcasters need to be freed from the control of corporate cartels. Since the Telecommunications Act of 1996 there has been a parade of media mergers and over 4,000 radio stations have been bought up in the United States, while television networks are now in the hands of huge corporations like General Electric, Viacom, Disney, and Rupert Murdoch's News Corporation. Murdoch also controls large portions of the television and newspaper media in Great Britain, Australia, and elsewhere. Corporate media have done their best to hide corporate scandals and to downplay or distort any protests against corporations.

11. Material reported as coming from "think tanks" needs to be labeled with information about the bias of such sources. They generally claim to be nonpartisan research organizations, while actually slanting their writings toward one party or against other and showing little evidence of any objective research despite their tax-exempt status.

12. Because the mainstream media coverage of protests against WTO, IMF and World Bank abuses, such as at Seattle and Genoa and at the Republican and Democratic conventions, distorts the events (stressing violent actions and ignoring the message of peaceful protesters), it is important that independent media be able to continue reporting on www.indymedia.org and other Internet sites. The Internet itself must be kept free of control by governments and private monopolies.

13. Local organizations should be allowed to operate low-power radio as another means of conveying information independent of the media cartel. So far, the lobbying power of the National Association of Broadcasters with Congress and the Federal Communications Commission

(FCC) has blocked such efforts in the United States on spurious claims of interference with commercial radio signals.

14. Writing letters to the editor of publications sometimes is a way of circulating information that is ignored in the news columns. Editors try to exhibit fairness by publishing letters expressing varied view, including ones disagreeing with the paper's editorial policy. Such letters may have little impact, but they can start people thinking.

15. It is important for individuals to get information "outside the box"—the television box, that is. The "infotainment" supplied by the media cartel tends to structure people's thinking in a way that makes them avid consumers with short attention spans and little interest in matters of substance. It builds and reinforces stereotypes (that some scientists label "memes" or "holodynes") that prejudice a person's thinking and reaction to new information.

16. There are dangers in the recent trend to protect corporate profits with the concept of "intellectual property" embodied in copyright extension long beyond the lifetime of the innovators, overreaching software patents, and international enforcement agreements. Unreasonable copyright and patent provisions need to be reversed.

> *"Public opinion in this country is everything."*
>
> —Abraham Lincoln, speech, Columbus Ohio, 1859

> *"You can fool some of the people all of the time, and all of the people some of the time, but you cannot fool all of the people all of the time."*
>
> —Abraham Lincoln, speech, 1856

> *"The great masses of the people in the very bottom of their heart tend to be corrupted rather than consciously and purposely evil...therefore, in view of the primitive simplicity of their minds, they more easily fall a victim to a big lie than to a little one, since*

they themselves lie in little things, but would be ashamed of lies that were too big."

—Adolph Hitler, as quoted by William Blum in "Rogue State, A Guide to the World's Only Superpower," p. 11.

6

The Spiritual Basis for Sustainable Living

✦

(based on a summary by Richard Gauthier in Poland)

This chapter is a discussion of humankind's relationship with nature and the universe. It holds there is more to life than material possessions and indulgences. Although people differ in their beliefs about creation and divinity, most recognize goals and principles greater than personal satisfaction.

There are two sides to capitalistic materialism. It has had enormous success because it is furthering the progress of humankind. It permits the emancipation of humanity from the "prison of the earth," our natural condition. Scientific advances and the initiatives spurred by the profit motive have raised the standard of living for many above mere survival.

However, excesses of greed and technology can undermine quality of life. Because excesses of capitalism have isolated humanity from nature by making it pleasure seeking, self-indulgent, and controlling, we must reestablish our relationship with nature and be aware of the unity in creation.

To make the world a better place is the ambition of many people. Perhaps it comes from an innate feeling that life has a purpose and from a desire to give significance to one's presence on this planet. Such motives need to be awakened if the necessary global reforms are to be achieved. They are strengthened when people recognize powers in the universe greater than their own private interests.

Some moralists deny that there can be any good without belief in a supernatural being—sometimes in the precise form that they conceive God. They claim that non-believers can only seek their own pleasure regardless of harm to others and that without religion there can be nothing but evil. (They tend to treat agnostics the same as atheists, although agnostics honestly admit they don't know while atheists flatly deny the possibility of God.)

Facts tend to contradict that assertion, as one can easily find good and bad in both the devout and the nonbelievers. When thinking of unselfish service to others, names that quickly come to mind include Dr. Albert Schweitzer, Mother Teresa, and Mahatma Gandhi, all motivated by traditional religion, and many others could be cited. Yet history is full of contrary examples, ostensibly devout people claiming God approved of their mistreatment of others, as in the case of the Crusades, the Inquisition, and apologists for slavery. Current examples include both sides in Northern Ireland, Hindus and Muslims in India and Pakistan, and Jewish and Arab extremists in the Middle East. It is also clear that commercial and colonial interests have often tired to cloak their selfish objectives behind a façade of religion.

Among people rejecting conventional religion many have been admirable, as far back as Socrates, who was put to death in 399 BC for "neglect of the gods whom the city worships." A later example is Voltaire, a satirist and crusader against tyranny, bigotry, and cruelty. Like Thomas Jefferson and others, he was a "deist," one who believes in a supreme being but rejects religious orthodoxy. There is no shortage of villainous nonbelievers, either, obviously including Stalin and Mao Tse-tung.

People of different religions and of no religion can cooperate together for good. What is important is for them to recognize freedom of thought. Unfortunately, when religion is authoritarian (whether fundamentalist Christian, orthodox Judaism, strict Islam, or any other) it elevates faith over thought and uses fear of damnation to enforce its particular set of beliefs. That would suggest God provided brains but does not want them to be used.

With respect for the thoughts of other people, it is possible to draw on sources of inspiration from many cultures and from such inner resources as one may find. Although people differ in their beliefs about creation and divinity, most recognize goals and principles greater than personal satisfaction. Some scientific studies purport to have found a spiritual center in the brain that appears to have been affected by meditation and prayer as measured by brain wave scans.

The following is thought to express the consensus of the participants in creating this book:

1. Spirituality aids the elevation, evolution, and progress of all beings.

2. Spirituality conceives of human beings as more than physical bodies, having individual souls, selves, minds and/or personalities.

3. The goal of human life is seen to be realization of soul or self as one with infinity.

4. Attainment of that goal represents fulfillment of all human longings.

5. Conscious efforts to attain the infinite source may be called spiritual practices.

6. Spiritual teachings, which provide guidance for spiritual practices, may come from internal (intuitional) and/or external sources.

7. Spirituality is universal and can be practiced at some level by anyone.

8. There is an attraction and family relationship among all human beings and other living beings due to their common spiritual origin and common spiritual destination.

9. One has a duty in life to work for spiritual progress and to help others progress.

10. Human beings require basic physical necessities of life and helpful guidance in order to progress physically, mentally and spiritually.

11. Society should make sure that all have access to these necessities and the opportunity to make such progress.

12. All beings, including animals and plants, should be treated with love and respect.

13. In harming others, one harms oneself. In helping others, one helps oneself.

14. Everyone has the right to protect themselves and others from harm.

15. Deep changes can come from within the individual and then spread to others.

16. A positive example is the best teacher.

17. The human intellect must be liberated from narrow and dogmatic ideas and sentiments.

7

Civil Society and Alternative Life Styles

✦

(based on a summary by Bill Ellis in Maine, USA)

This chapter examines how directly democratic organization of society can bring people into better harmony with other life on the planet while avoiding the damage caused by large-scale exploitation of the environment. Some of the thoughts presented here were inspired by E. F. Schumacher's 1973 book, *Small is Beautiful,* and the lecture Bill Ellis gave before the E. F. Schumacher Society in 1998.

Today the people of the world are challenged with unprecedented problems as improper care for the earth's ecological systems threatens the planet's life support system and has brought us to the brink of collapse. At the same time soaring population places increasing demands on these fragile and interconnected systems.

In addition, technological advances have made human labor forces increasingly irrelevant to the production of goods and thus divorced from the financial markets. As civilization proceeds from the industrial age into the age of knowledge millions of people may be left behind with no means of sustenance.

As detailed in previous chapters, the powerful are proceeding down the path of globalization, disregarding the needs of people and the environment while enhancing the fortunes of the few (see Chapter 4).

This has resulted in most of the world's wealth being concentrated while many millions of others worldwide suffer from unbearable poverty with hardships bordering on deliberate inhumane treatment.

Under what some refer to as the "dominator paradigm" prevailing over thousands of years, economic needs supercede the natural order of earth needs. Modern attempts to increase food production by the sale and use of chemical fertilizers, pesticides and herbicides, mono-cropping, and intensive meat production are largely responsible for increasing desertification as a result of worldwide topsoil losses. Since civilization itself is dependent upon the topsoil on which it rests, we are digging the foundation out from under our home.

Now, inadequately tested bioengineering practices (genetically modified products), saturation of live stock with antibiotics, irradiation, and use of hormones to increase milk production introduce possible new dangers.

As these problems become more evident, millions of individuals around the world are beginning to question the stability and security of our present systems and join with like-minded others to explore the situation. As a result there is a movement toward the creation of "sustainable living" societies based on decentralized financial systems, governance through bioregionalism, and lessening of dependence on world trade.

Such people are sometimes described as "inner directed," "cultural creatives" and/or "integral culturists." They believe that competition is antithetical to sustainable living and insist on cooperation. A turn in the direction of sustainable living requires that society examine its old thought patterns and adopt lifestyles that more nearly fit the needs of today. Although such sustainable local or regional communities tend to be restricted in size, they can be linked with other communities in cooperative networks that have unlimited potential.

A vision of direct democracy—participatory democracy not under hierarchical control—was offered in a 1982 TRANET (transnational network tranet@rangeley.org) editorial. Made possible by new technology and concepts, a future world government can be pictured as a network of networks in which each individual has multiple paths available to provide for his or her well-being and to influence world affairs. Various members would associate for special projects or issues but without any bureaucracy demanding action or conformity.

The cells of this future of governance are emerging on many fronts. There are innovative social techniques such as Local Employment Trading Systems (LETS), CoHousing, Homesteading, Intentional Communities, local scrips, food co-ops, Employee Stock Option Plans (ESOPs), Community Supported Agriculture (CSAs), and many others. Also hundreds of thousands of Grass Roots Organizations (GROs) are springing up around the world, solving local problems with local skills and local resources. They are no longer waiting for governments or corporations to solve their local problems and develop their local potentials.

In the physical world, atoms, molecules, or cells, in sufficient numbers tend to form networks and special conglomerations. Simpler entities combine into larger ones. Elisabet Sahtouris, in *Earth Dance: A Living System of Evolution,* suggests that the human body with its cells organized into organs, and organs organized into a living being is a perfect metaphor for society. Ervin Laszlo and the Budapest Group carry the concept even further with their concept of "General Evolution."

The same pattern is being followed by civil society and the burgeoning GROs are following that pattern. Also, to support the network of GROs, Grassroots Support Organizations (GRSOs) are forming, most often by middle class professionals and technicians who recognize the inequities engendered by the current economic-political system. GRSOs reach out to give in-kind assistance and to legitimize the actions of the peasants and disenfranchised in their bids for empowerment and local self-reliance. Techniques, technologies, information, and service from the industrial countries are supplied through links created by international non-governmental organizations (INGOs).

Julie Fisher in *The Road from Rio* describes a worldwide network of GROs, GRSOs and INGOs in terms that fit perfectly into chaos and complexity theory. A living body of networked organizations has emerged to fill the niche produced by dysfunctional post-colonial governments. Interdependent social cells have developed organs assuming specialized functions that serve the whole social/political body that promises better life for the people in developing countries and the whole Earth. The natural laws being revealed in chaos, complexity, and Gaian theories, are working on the social level.

As Elise Boulding pointed out in her book, *Building a Global Civic Culture*, the heart of a new world governance has already formed. Through the revelations of science, an understanding of the cosmic process is slowly emerging. With this new understanding, humanity may be participating in the creation of a sustainable and lasting civilization based on citizen participation in local community organizations—a Gaian global governance.

Modern forms of democracy are relatively new in human existence, and have never reached perfect form. Classical studies examine Athenian and Roman experience, in which important parts of the population were excluded from government. The prevailing system into the 18th Century was absolute monarchy, based on the "divine right of kings." Neither churches nor governments were friendly to the idea that common people could rule themselves, nor even participate in government. The ideas of voting, representation, legislating, human rights, politics, constitutions, or social contracts were little more than hazy academic notions.

A landmark step was the curtailment of royal power in the Magna Carta imposed on King John of England in 1215 by the barons, which led, after much travail, to the modern constitutional monarchy in Britain, where traditions are preserved but power is effectively in the elected parliament. Over the years constitutional monarchies in which royal powers are limited have been established in other European countries.

By the 18th Century, masses of people recognized that they were missing out on many of the benefits that their toil had created. "It was the best of times, and the worst of times," as later described in Charles Dickens' *The Tale of Two Cities*. The American Revolution in 1776 and the French Revolution in 1789 (interrupted by the emperor Napoleon and a restoration of Bourbon kings until another revolt in 1848) ushered in new concepts of democracy.

Modern democracy came into being within what has been called the "Dominator Paradigm" based on the Genesis creation story holding that the earth was created for the use and domination of man. This was further developed by Greek philosophers. Then the Medieval Church and its "chain of being" put man near the top of a hierarchy, followed by women, children, other races, animals, plants, and the earth. In 1776 Adam Smith's laissez-faire economic theories held that the best for all would be produced by the self-interest of each through the operation of an "invisible hand."

The American colonies had assumed a degree of self-government under the British Crown, but voting rights were usually denied women, blacks, Catholics, Jews, slaves, and anyone lacking substantial land holdings. Probably no more than one third of the adult free men could vote. Office holding was even more restricted, based on property ownership. Many of these limitations continued after the revolution. In spite of subsequent extended suffrage to blacks, women, and all citizens, the voice of the people has been steadily eroded as corporations have grown in size and power. (See Chapter 2.)

It is now possible to enter a new phase of democracy due to expanding civil society, modern technology, and a new scientific understanding of how evolution works. The theories of Chaos, Complexity and Gaia have a suggested a "Gaian Paradigm" in which the earth and all the cosmos evolve as a single unit, system, or "holon." Every entity of the universe is a unit composed of smaller units and embedded in larger units. The whole is dependent on every part, and each part is dependent on the whole, evolving in harmony and unison. Simple units combine to form more complex ones, which in turn combine in ever more complex forms.

Biological evolution is the most obvious example of the tendency toward the ordering of simple entities into more complex systems. Flexibility is one of the cardinal biological principles of evolution. Without flexibility a life form is not sustainable, it cannot change to meet new conditions. But governments, like corporations, have been organized within the Dominator Paradigm—good management means rigid order controlled from the top.

That idea is contradicted by a best-selling book "Birth of the Chaordic Age" by Dee W. Heck, retired head of the Visa worldwide credit card company composed of more than 20,000 banks. He has been acclaimed for his successful management style that emphasizes choosing capable subordinates and letting them solve problems with their unique abilities instead of micro-managing them. He believes that successful systems thrive on the edge of chaos with just enough order to give them pattern, and calls this concept "chaordic" from a combination of chaos and order.

If society is to meet the challenges that face it, it needs to live closer to the edge of chaos. It must welcome a degree of disorder. Democracy since its modern inception has suffered from its self-guilt of being inefficient. The Gaian Paradigm sees democracy in a very different light. The seeming weaknesses of democracy are its strength. The theories of Gaia, Chaos, and Complexity suggest that self-organizing on the edge of chaos is natural law. It requires the messy flexibility inherent in democracy.

The rise of civil society, the burgeoning of GROs, the growth of social innovation, community involvement in meeting their own needs, are all parts of the progressive agenda provided by nature. We may not see clearly today the final organization that will emerge if we continue to build decentralized autonomous communities linked together in worldwide mutual aid. But, that is the way of cosmic evolution as it is seen from the new worldview. It portends the emergence of a new phase of democracy—one in which people in community at the grassroots have a direct input to all decisions which affect their lives—a new form of global governance.

8

Education as an Essential Tool for Finding Solutions

✦

(based on a summary by Bill Ellis in Maine, USA)

This chapter considers the limitations of traditional education and proposes lifetime learning that enables people to adapt to rapidly changing conditions. Such learning is less structured than traditional systems and reflects scientific discoveries about the non-linear functioning of the human brain. It turns away from the "dominator paradigm" that claims nature exists for exploitation by man in favor of the "gaian paradigm" that emphasizes interaction of living things. From neighborhood day care centers to home-schooling cooperatives, to senior hostels, new clubs and centers are creating the learning opportunities that could grow into a more human and humane learning system.

For democracy to work best the public should be literate and well educated in order to recognize the truth or falsity of political arguments. That is not an argument for voter qualifications because the individual, regardless of high or low intellectual development, is a better judge than anyone else of what is good for his or her welfare. However, it is an argument for providing universal education.

The political corruption and media concentration already discussed, as well as subsidized propaganda machines disguised as research organizations or "think tanks," make it all the more important for people to judge information critically. The prevalence of misinformation, including improper influences on university teaching, is exposed in *"Playing with the Numbers: How So-called Experts Mislead Us about the Economy"* by Richard A. Stimson (Westchester Press, 1999, www.stimson.homestead.com).

Particularly alarming is the incursion of commercial influences in the schools, especially in the United States, where commercial innovations often start. Endowments and research grants have been used by wealthy individuals and corporations to warp university activities. Athletic departments have come to overshadow academics as contracts with shoe companies and other equipment suppliers inflate the pay of coaches far above professors and even academic administrators. Most horrifying is that many school systems, in exchange for donations of electronic equipment, expose pupils in the classroom to mandatory television commercials from Channel One (although others have laudably refused it).

The growth of free public schools in the United States in the 19th century has been credited for much of the progress experienced by that country. The Industrial Age, spreading from a few factories in the Northeast, required that farmers and tradesmen learn new skills and new lifestyles. Their lives were controlled by the assembly line and the factory whistle instead of the weather and planting seasons. They were attracted by wages and urban conveniences not found in rural areas.

To produce new generations of workers with industrial skills and a sense of discipline the new education system was created and, not wholly incidentally, gave the young a background of information that helped them become useful citizens of a democracy. This system served as a model for universal education in other advanced countries. The provision of government-financed higher education for veterans of World War II was a further documented success.

Since then, there has been much more criticism of U.S. education. *The Index of Leading Cultural Indicators* by William Bennett reported that violent crime, allowing for population growth, was four to five times greater in 1994 than in 1960, births among unmarried teenage girls were three times higher, and teenage suicide was nearly three times higher. SAT scores in math dropped 20 points and verbal scores 50 points during the same years.

The National Science Foundation ranked the performance in physical sciences of United States 4th to 12th graders in eleventh world position, after six European and three Asian countries and Australia, with England and Hong Kong heading the list.

It has frequently been asserted by evangelical (fundamentalist) Christians that society's problems began when the Supreme Court banned prayer in the public schools. More correctly stated, the court banned religious indoctrination, including formal prayer, as a violation of the Constitution. Nothing stops a student from praying privately to God, and it is safe to say that this often occurs at exam time and in athletic competition. Whether mandatory daily prayers formerly observed in the schools resulted in better behavior and learning is debatable, but there are certainly other explanations for the changes that have been observed.

Until school psychologists, teachers, and teachers colleges began to stress peer approval, nobody had thought there could be any such thing as over-achievement. But then some school psychologists flabbergasted parents by asking whether they weren't worried that their children were ahead of the rest of the class!

Some educational weaknesses have a long history and certainly began before the 1960s. It is possible they expanded in that decade, but some risky ideas based on quack psychology and/or untried educational theories also surfaced in the 1970s and 1980s, such as:

- Report cards that emphasize psychological opinions.

- Stress on social skills and conformity with peers.

- Reading by "look and say" rather than phonics.

- "New Math" involving set theory and non-decimal systems.

- De-emphasizing geography and history.

- Inflating grades to encourage "self-esteem."

- Weakening disciplinary measures available to teachers.

- Discouraging parents from spanking children.

- Social promotion.

However well intentioned these ideas, they all tended to undermine the schools' main mission of providing fundamental skills and subject-matter knowledge. Some excellent work is done in teacher training institutions, but some ill-considered ideas also gain currency and can become dangerous fads.

Perhaps it is time for another revolution in education, as we face a new age of transition. Factories no longer dominate employment in the U.S. and many other developed nations. For example, only 3% or 4% of Americans now work on assembly lines. Traditional emphasis on training for jobs has suppressed people's natural curiosity and the joy of learning for its mere satisfaction. The appreciation and love for life for all individuals is dependent on their grasp of knowledge of the world and the world of knowledge.

Neither in the economically powerful G8 nations, nor in the towns of less developed countries where multinational corporations have opened factories, is there the traditional pattern where father goes to work, mother keeps the home, and the children attend school. Today's world is a complex maze of ever-changing networks within networks.

Communications have made it possible for books like this one to be written collectively by people living thousands of miles apart and never meeting one another face to face. Each person is a node of a network, simultaneously enmeshed in a myriad of interlinked communities and virtual communities. As social relations have become more complex, they have also become more changeable.

Within the old social/economic/education system one could expect to learn in school all that was needed to hold a job. Graduation was regarded as one's passport for a lifetime in the world of work. That is no longer true. Students in societies of advanced technology are told that they must expect to change jobs and careers several times in their lives. In other cultures, the way of life that had not changed for many generations may become impossible to follow because of manmade or natural changes in the environment.

It is no longer enough for schools to pass on the educational content needed for a job. It becomes far more important to develop versatility and the ability to adapt to new challenges. The learning system of the future must find ways to help people continue their education and intellectual growth.

The past few decades have seen an erosion of the traditional nuclear family (if it ever was), but the need for "belonging" to an extended family is still a basic need for all humans. A new form of intentional community is emerging that, with nurturing, can become the soul of society. Cooperative Community Life-Long Learning Centers (CCL-LLCs)—or Community Learning and Information Centers (CLICs)—can provide that critical social need. Information can be found at: http://www.creatinglearningcommunities.org/resources, http://www.clic-manlius.org, http://www.tii-kokopellispirit.org, and http://www.ranui org.nz.

Society today demands attention to interaction with other people. As business focuses more on information transfer than on the production of material goods, the social relationships take on a greater importance, involving who transmits information to whom and how. Social relationships are becoming more and more an element of working relationships.

Our interrelationships in the social world are not about just our economic well being. They are about the deeper more fundamental basic need of "belonging"–of caring and being cared for—of self-respect and self-actualization. Humans are again hearing that small inner voice that asks the questions such as 'Why am I here?" and 'What is the purpose of life?"

From the viewpoint of the individual, each is a node in the web of being, like a star reaching out from the most intimate connections to friends and family and branching out through other nodes to communities, society, and the natural world. As the branching stars get further and further away from the individual the links become ever weaker, and their importance to the individual seems ever more and more remote. It is those nearest and strongest links that provide the more important interconnections for the person.

This is the place of families and communities, where personal gain is sublimated to the common good and where economics and materialism come second. It is the place where we exist for one another and for the wellbeing of the whole—where we gladly forego the luxuries of life for friendship, companionship, and the wellbeing of others—the place where we "belong." This is the common meaning of "community."

Communities come in many colors. Often the word is restricted to people living in a particular area, and/or people with a common interest—and certainly these characteristics help create community solidarity. In the age of instant worldwide communications the forming of fraternal linking in virtual communities is becoming part of our social being. And for ages past humanity's basic need to "belong" has been met, in part at least, by nations, religions, and other forms of social relations.

In fact, every person wears a coat of many colors, being a member of various communities. For many people even the family is of secondary importance to other communal ties, such as the gang, the secret society, or the cult. If the need for "belonging" is not met in socially beneficial ways, somewhere, it may break out in violence, often deadly, against coworkers, schoolmates, and/or adherence to anti-social communities, as the need for community is a universal need.

New communities are developing with more openness than the extended-family communities of the agrarian age and the industrial age which prided themselves on closeness and independence of others while rejecting and disparaging values, celebrations, lifestyles, and beliefs from outside the group. Communities are now beginning to reach out in cooperation beyond the limits of family, tribe, nation, and religion. Differences in food, dress, ritual, lifestyles, and values are found to make life interesting and often lead to fads. This is the world for which the learning system must prepare its future citizens.

The Future of Learning-The Future of Community

As Horace Mann recognized in 1870, and as modern science confirms today, the earliest years in a human's life are the ones in which life patterns are set. Crucial to the citizens of the future is the capacity to change and to continue lifelong learning. The radically changing society requires citizens who can change with the times. Future citizens must be prepared from their earliest days, and throughout their lives, to be the creators of continually evolving webs of being.

Some of us have a vision of "Learning Communities" that will replace government schools and will know how to change with the times. They will also provide learning opportunities for all of their citizens. Libraries, museums, parks, farms, factories, businesses, homes, and the streets will be the new milieu for learning. Learners will see gaining new skills and knowledge as their central purpose for being. Material luxuries will become of secondary importance to social and cultural well being.

There are at least three ways of looking at the term "Learning Communities": (1) communities that learn, (2) communities that provide learning opportunities, and (3) communities of learners.

Communities That Learn

First, "Learning Communities" implies communities that are learning and continually evolving, a connotation most relevant because all of society is in a state of transition. The European-American world was built on what is sometimes called the *Dominator Paradigm*, based on the view that the earth, including women, children, animals, plants, and the physical universe, was made for the domination and use of man.

Science has revealed a different cosmos—one that evolves holonistically; that is, a world of interlocked and interdependent systems or holons within each other that make up a new worldview we call the *Gaian Paradigm*. It conceives of humans as imbedded in turn in family, community, society, and nature. The wellbeing of each individual depends on the wellbeing of the larger holons in which he is imbedded as well as the small holons that are his parts. Thus the wellbeing of each of us is dependent on our evolving community which equally is dependent on the learning growth of each of us.

Communities That Provide Learning Opportunities

Another related connotation for "learning community" is a community that provides lifelong learning experiences for all its citizens, each of whom participates in the evolution of the community and learns from every aspect of the community.

Libraries, museums, farms, fields, forests, factories, businesses, parks, mountains, lakes, and the streets are where we learn. Citizens of all ages are provided opportunities to increase their skills and their knowledge. Future citizens are not locked away in schools separated from family, community, society and nature. They are active parts of the every evolving community and participate throughout their lives in the affairs of the community.

Communities of Learners

The third description of Learning Communities, and perhaps the most meaningful, is as communities of self-learners. Modern brain research reveals every input from our senses is sorted and harmonized with our existing memory in a single neural network that is distributed throughout the brain. This implies that each brain is unique and new knowledge cannot be forced into the brains of different individuals at the same time in the same way.

Within this context learning communities provide systems of socialization, not merely in terms of companionship and meeting needs for "belonging" but through learning about others as well as learning with others. The learning community is the foundation on which the larger community and society can be built.

Conclusion

We are inescapably communities of learners, but seldom consciously created and often ephemeral. In the past decade or so there has been a rapid increase in grassroots groups taking charge of their own learning—learning circles, book clubs, home school support groups, learning libraries, and many other forms of collaborative learning. Civil Society is becoming a third leg of governance along with the nation state and the corporate network, as grass roots organizations (GROs) are solving local problems with local skills and local resources.

With the continuance of these trends, there could be an age in which economic and material values are overtaken by the values of humanity, cooperation, and mutual aid. The creation of learning communities can be the key to the wellbeing of all.

Meanwhile, the conventional elementary and secondary educational systems, which will not immediately disappear, stand in need of serious reform, as also do the universities.

9

Summary and Conclusions

Progress or pitfalls?

Beyond the daily disasters in the news there is a huge global crisis. Changes are coming faster then ever—some good, but too many bad. Science and invention have opened up possibilities hardly dreamed of before—also new dangers.

On the plus side, technology has made mind-boggling progress to provide cheap and rapid communication around the globe, but the Internet has also been used for spreading "spam," computer viruses, pornography, and hate messages, and to carry terrorists' coded plans. Automation has made it almost unnecessary for most people to think, but is that a good thing? Networking also opens up the possibility for saboteurs to do catastrophic damage to public utilities and systems. And what happens when there are programming errors and there is no provision for human intervention?

Medical science has greatly extended human life spans and new discoveries offer relief from many diseases, but rapidly increasing population raises new problems. How large a total population can be supported by the natural resources of the planet? Agricultural progress has made it possible to produce enough food for everyone, although flaws of distribution still result in shortages in some places while there are surpluses being destroyed elsewhere. World population has grown far beyond what Malthus in the 18th Century thought possible, but there must be some limit. Perhaps pollution, traffic congestion, and the stress of crowded living will reach the limit before science runs out of ways to provide food. At the same time, recent developments in food production have produced harmful effects whose full extent is yet unknown, especially with regard to chemical adulteration, genetic experimentation, and unsanitary conditions in food processing plants.

More varieties of entertainment are available than ever before, with sounds and images reaching everywhere, reflected from satellites as well as travelling on fiber-optic cable, in a wide swath of the broadcast spectrum, and by ordinary circuits. People, especially the younger generations, are seldom without some form of music or talk—nor are they lacking in propaganda and/or advertising messages. The quality of entertainment, however, has declined, catering to the lowest common denominator, and news has to travel the same channels, often being selected and distorted to serve entertainment and commercial purposes. Time for quiet thought and meditation has become rare in many environments.

Countless international bodies exist, many within the United Nations framework, with the ostensible purpose of solving world problems, but too often they are corrupted by political and commercial considerations. Ancient evils continue with potential for harm on a greater scale. War, ethnic clashes, racial hatred, corrupt governments, fraud, embezzlement, street crime, police brutality, torture, assassinations, wrongful imprisonment, and even slavery continue. Air, water, and soil are polluted, forests and wetlands are desecrated, food is adulterated, people are exposed to unproven genetically modified crops, and workers are endangered on the job—all because of greed for more profit.

The dark side of accelerated technical progress is accelerated peril. Ancient disasters could wipe out a civilization. Modern disasters could end the human species and maybe all life on this planet. This possibility has hovered over us since the invention of the atomic bomb. Now there is also widespread fear of biological and chemical weapons. These hazards are spread not only by ill will but also because of profits to arms merchants and war financiers.

The struggle for self-government

Democracy holds the best-known hope for safe passage through these times of danger. For it to be effective, people must know and understand the events around them. As people who have never been allowed to vote before obtain this opportunity, they brave great dangers and persevere through inconvenience to make their choices at the ballot box. Later generations may take it for granted and risk losing control of their own fate through careless indifference.

Major decisions about the course of world events are often being made without the knowledge or consent of the people who will suffer the consequences. The people who control the world's largest commercial and financial corporations, however, have every opportunity to know about and influence these actions—whether the decisions are being made in the secret energy policy conferences held by U.S. Vice President Cheney with energy company executives, or the secret rulings of the World Trade Organization (WTO), or other international bodies dominated by financial interests with little or no representation of organizations working for the public interest.

The privileged and powerful of the world meet each other in such decision-making bodies, as well as in G-8 summits, the exclusive Bilderberg, the Trilateral Commission, and the Council on Foreign Relations. Increasingly they live in fortified mansions, walled and gated communities, surrounded by armed guards, and protected by secret police, even in countries that purport to be democratic. They are mostly out of touch with the people whose lives they largely control.

They tell each other and the public that their globalization policies are for the benefit of everyone. The objections raised in this book, and by most of the peaceful protesters at international meetings around the world, are not to globalization itself (we are using the global Internet to write this book) but to undemocratic, exploitive, and monopolistic methods being used. There is a tacit recognition of this in various references to "the current form of globalization" in UNCTAD's June 2002 report on the poverty trap (www.unctad.org).

Where governments are intended to be answerable to the people, it should be possible to correct economic and environmental problems by legislation and regulation. Although some 58% of the world's people live in countries that are counted as democracies, that leaves 42% with no representative government. Even purported democracies are often far from perfect.

The solution for some people is to form self-sustaining cooperative communities with respect for nature and freedom from outside control. As much merit as there may be in such life styles, they are not to the taste of everyone and the communities must be concerned whether governments and developers will refrain from interfering with them. The experience of many indigenous cultures as oil and mining companies moved in with collaboration of corrupt governments suggests that government cannot just be ignored.

Likewise, anarchy (essentially meaning to do away with all government) could only work among idealistic people who would discipline themselves, which is not the state of evolution humanity has achieved yet. Greed and "might makes right" are still strong elements of the world we live in.

Since the forces working to seize power and wealth oppose democratic reforms, social justice, human rights, and sustainable local economies, citizens must never tire of exercising their rights. "Eternal vigilance is the price of liberty." There is a constant battle to restrain politicians from accepting bribes and special interests from offering them to gain unfair advantages.

The benefits of democracy can only be obtained if all parties, including new ones and small start-ups, can compete for voter approval. This requires that they be able to get on the ballot and that their message can reach the public. Honest counts and fairly drawn voting districts are essential, and there can be advantages to preference voting, instant run-offs, proportional representation, initiatives, referendums, and the none-of–the-above option.

Political action at the global level becomes necessary because reform efforts locally can be thwarted when multinational corporations threaten to move business and jobs to another more permissive jurisdiction. This calls for joint actions by nations and/or stronger world government. Democratic control must be included to prevent global tyranny.

The many territorial disputes of the world threaten peace and freedom. Self-determination should be the underlying principle, but each conflict raises unique problems that make solution difficult and slow. Respect for each other's traditions and beliefs is difficult but essential. Arms merchants and their political allies have worsened traditional conflicts, and development programs that have concentrated people in urban slums have increased frictions. As those conditions have become intolerable, desperate people have taken great risks to emigrate, creating new problems for the countries where they seek asylum or economic opportunity.

Devolution (the return of powers to smaller political units) has been applied in Britain and discussed elsewhere. The advantages of bringing decisions home from national bureaucracies to manageable local areas always needs to be weighed against the advantages of uniformity of law and opportunities over a wider area.

To build and nourish democratic political institutions, it is suggested that people work for social justice and environmental benefits, work against monopolistic trends, use demonstrations and legal action against wrongs, vote intelligently, engage in community efforts for public services and environmental protection, support regulatory protection of the public commons (air, water, parkland, etc.), hold polluters financially responsible for adverse externalities they cause, reform corporate charters to remove their unfair advantages over individuals, and promote more open and responsible forms of international institutions.

Using corporations to rule the world

Progress in political institutions is difficult because of the undue influence of big business and financial interests. Chief executive officers of large corporations are either among the ruling elite of the world or else well compensated to be their representatives. Compensation of CEOs in the U.S., which used to be about 40 times the average for blue-collar workers in 1960, had reached a 531-to-1 ratio in 2001. CEOs serve on each other's boards of directors, along with bankers, lawyers, accountants, and financial underwriters, all voting each other salaries, fees, bonuses, perks, pensions, stock options, and other benefits paid by the stockholders.

When the law requires stockholder approval of board actions, ordinary investors who own shares through mutual funds have their stock voted by fund managers without consulting them, and almost always in favor of whatever management proposes. If stockholders sue for misbehavior of management, the corporate officers customarily get their legal expenses paid from company funds.

The corporate scandals that began unfolding early in 2002 involving such large corporations as Enron, WorldCom, Global Crossing, Tyco, and Rite Aid, revealed that top management, legal advisors, and auditors used accounting tricks to hide losses and inflate profits. The perpetrators walked away with millions, while ordinary employees and investors were left holding the bag as stock prices plummeted.

Among those prominent in obtaining political favors for corporations are the so-called "defense industries." They are big political campaign contributors, and their top officials are in and out of government positions in cabinet departments or the military. The governments then help them sell weapons to other countries, the leading suppliers being, in order, the United States, Russia, France, Germany, Britain, China, and Italy.

The rulers of big corporations tend to get their way most of the time. On the world scene, global corporations (including global bankers and financial companies) dominate international agencies unrestrained by democratic safeguards. The World Bank, the International Monetary Fund (IMF), and the World Trade Organization (WTO) override democratic governments. The WTO has forced America and Europe to annul various health and environmental laws. Third world countries have been required to turn over public services and natural resources to private multinational corporations as conditions for international loans.

The buzz words for these loan conditions include "neo-liberal," "structural adjustments," and, ironically, "reform." In fact, these policies involve removing government protections of health, safety, workers' rights, and the environment. Reports of the World Bank and IMF have even admitted the failure of many of their programs that were supposed to benefit less developed countries, but so far these organizations have given only lip service to human and environmental protection. Similarly, the North American Free Trade Agreement (NAFTA) was supposed to protect workers rights and the environment through "side agreements," but no funds were provided.

Although corporations everywhere fight to escape regulation, European countries have retained more protections for workers, consumers, and the environment. In May 2002, the European Parliament in Brussels voted for new legislation holding companies and their board members responsible for their social and environmental performance in Europe and in developing countries.

In recent years, however, the social-democratic parties in Europe have sought a "Third Way" between the welfare state and the free market. Paradoxically, many people felt caught between government and corporate bureaucracies and threatened by immigration due to oppression and poverty in less prosperous countries—giving popular support to nationalistic parties proposing to close borders against immigration.

Another unexpected phenomenon of economic changes has been the reduction of time people have away from work, with consequences for family and community life. When women work outside the home by choice it represents growth of opportunity, but many women work for wages because of economic necessity. Many people work more than one job, none of which provide the fringe benefits that were associated with employment. Others are unemployed with reduced social assistance. In less developed countries widespread unemployment has occurred as traditional food sources have been usurped and/or polluted, driving populations to seek factory employment in the cities.

The growth of monopolies and cartels has accelerated as governments increasingly abandoned enforcement of antitrust laws and courts sided with the corporations. Although mergers are claimed to result in economies of scale, the benefits are often not realized due to bureaucracy in large businesses. In any event, business concentration destroys the competition of many suppliers that is essential to free markets à la Adam Smith. Large retailers like Wal-Mart can drive small retailers out of business with introductory price bargains then, when they have monopoly control of the market, put its prices back up.

Corporations have special characteristics that individuals do not have. Under U.S. law these include perpetual life, immunity from jail, a legal mandate for single-minded profit seeking, lack of size limits, and the power to combine or divide themselves as a means of escaping responsibility for actions of subsidiaries.

As the corporate oligarchy has increasingly dominated economic summits and international trade meetings, these conferences attended by public officials gravitate toward inaccessible sites guarded by armed forces to isolate them from any public objections. Peaceful protesters have been brutally treated on the pretext of controlling vandalism, when violence was often initiated by police or their *agents-provocateurs*.

Corporate subsidies, endowments, junkets, propaganda and pressures have been used to bring universities, research organizations, and judicial agencies to their way of thinking. The enormous power of corporations and their friends in government has been almost totally ignored in political science academic studies. Industrial causes of cancer receive little attention from cancer research organizations. Law schools receive strings-attached donations and judges are sent to luxury resorts for seminars where they are propagandized by advocates of *laissez-faire* economics.

By playing off one nation or locality against another, large businesses extract subsidies, privileges, tax breaks, and freedom from regulations concerning health, safety, employee rights, or pollution. Some corrupt national leaders accept money from corporations to help them drive people off their land into homeless city life while the land is poisoned by drilling and mining operations. The money usually goes into secret foreign bank accounts, along with proceeds of international loans. The corrupt tyrants live very well in exile if and when the populace rises up and expels them.

The economists usually quoted by the media tend to measure economic development (and progress) by gross domestic product (GDP), which only counts products and services that are sold for money. Housework, preparing home meals, bringing up children, do-it-yourself projects, and raising crops for family consumption are all treated as worthless, while transportation to work, hiring childcare, and restaurant meals, as well as wages for outside work, are included in GDP.

These and other statistical errors can make it appear that a nation's economy is improving while living conditions of most of the population are actually deteriorating. GDP also disregards harmful side effects to public health and the environment, and it says nothing about how widely or narrowly the national income is distributed.

Among the reasons for environmental harm is ignoring "externalities" such as pollution-caused illnesses, poisoning of food sources (such as fish in the streams and crops in the land), and hazards to employees. One suggested method of correcting this is "true-cost-pricing" where the government would require such costs to be included in prices, with proceeds to be use for overcoming the harmful effects.

Seriously harmful "external" costs imposed on people around the world include air and water pollution, contamination of food with persistent pesticides, fostering of drug-resistant bacteria by overuse of antibiotics on healthy livestock, recklessly injecting hormones into dairy cows, and experimenting on the public by promoting genetically modified foods before determining that they are safe. Air pollution has made the natural problems of allergies much worse and contributed to the increase of cancer. Dioxin (a byproduct of chlorine bleaching of paper) and endosulfan (a pesticide) are well known problems too often ignored.

Corporations responsible for such lethal "externalities" attempt to escape responsibility by demanding absolute proof that the harmful effects are due to their operation rather than other sources, and by trumpeting exaggerated estimates of the cost they assert would be passed on to consumers.

To give them their due, in many ways capitalist enterprises use resources efficiently. A reformed capitalism that sustains democratic values rather than restrains them and includes all the costs to the environment would include giving workers a legitimate right to bargain with corporations, breaking up powerful trusts, holding corporate officers criminally responsible for corporate crimes, and making it illegal for corporations to participate in any political process.

The arguments made for private enterprise (often called "free markets" although the markets are dominated by monopolies and cartels) usually confuse the issue by equating democracy with capitalism. Likewise, mergers are trumpeted as beneficial for efficiency and convenience of consumers, when events frequently demonstrate the opposite. Big corporations tend to misuse their powers, but small and middle-sized companies (and entrepreneurs) give opportunities to individuals, producing more innovation, new products, and new jobs than the giants.

Employee ownership of businesses should be encouraged, thus guarding against shortsighted policies of absentee ownership, and banks must not be allowed to dictate the selection of management. Perhaps the best choice is a "mixed system" in which private businesses, producer cooperatives, consumer cooperatives, and government agencies all play their part.

Small businesses competing by Adam Smith rules are fine, and if they so please their customers that they grow large, so be it. What is wrong is when businesses combine to stifle competition and improperly influence government. Corporations are NOT persons, and should not be given even more rights than individuals. Limited liability without responsibility has caused much of the trouble we see today.

The top 200 corporations' combined sales exceed the combined economies of all countries except the biggest 10. Between 1983 and 1999, the profits of the Top 200 firms grew 362.4 percent, while the number of people they employ grew by only 14.4 percent. Such a trend cannot be healthy for the global economy.

Communication smothered by media cartel

Business concentration is bad in all industries that should be competitive, but it is especially harmful for communications media because it imposes commercial censorship that can be as bad as government censorship. In January 2002 *The Nation* published a special issue summarizing the holdings of the "Big Ten" members of the media cartel ranging in annual revenues from AT&T's $555 billion and General Electric's $130 billion down to Bertelsmann's $17 billion and News Corporation's $12 billion. The chart showed many joint ventures and percentage shares of ownership involving several of the ten companies.

The Big Ten generally include both the studios that produce content and channels that disseminate it. Entertainment dominates information for these companies, who own film studios and libraries, as well as many cinema theater chains. The world is split into six regions with DVD discs and players that are incompatible with those in other regions. Similarly, the incompatibility of television systems (and camcorders) in different parts of the world serves commercial interests at the expense of public convenience. Most of these companies are also deeply involved in distribution of popular music.

The U.S. Telecommunications Reform Act of 1996, overwhelmingly supported by both major parties, effectively removed virtually all limits in the communications and entertainment industries. Congress also extended patents and copyrights, allowing firms like Disney to profit from artistic work long after the originator is dead.

In the print media category there is also great concentration with most of the same players, including AOL/Time-Warner, Bertelsmann, and Rupert Murdoch's News Corporation. Control of newspapers and magazines has been merged into huge chains, and only a few companies control book publishing and retailing.

The Internet also involves the Big Ten, as well as Microsoft, which has a virtual monopoly of computer operating systems and web browsers and has been held in violation of the U.S. antitrust laws. As in the case of bio-piracy, patent laws have been applied far beyond their original intent, so that not just software code but even the method of achieving goals—elementary mathematical applications and concepts—have been patented.

The domination of media by big business has stifled information about health hazards such as dioxin, bovine growth hormones, nuclear radiation pollution, and genetically modified food products. During political campaigns the media concentrate on personalities and trivia while excluding non-establishment candidates from television debates and generally ignoring substantial political issues. (www.projectcensored.org) (www.fair.org)

Television and the press in the U.S. have almost completely ignored various strange and suspicious circumstances described in British and French media concerning the September 11, 2001, terrorist attacks in New York and Washington, obeying warnings from the White House to "be very careful."

Even school classrooms are not immune from commercialism, with pupils being forced to watch a daily half-hour of advertising-saturated programming in exchange for electronic equipment donated to the school (while soft drink companies are sold exclusive rights to push their sugary products and athletic shoe companies dominate sports programs).

Information media (including newspapers, magazines, books, television, radio, digital communication, and cinema) must be freed from censorship by government or commercial cartels, the latter being broken up under antitrust laws. Private companies should not be able to own and sell monopolies of broadcast spectrum—these should be periodically auctioned by governments subject to fair operation in the public interest or cancellation of the license, and the license should not be transferable as property.

Broadcasters should be required to provide a fair balance of opposing opinions, especially during election campaigns, with a reasonable amount of free time to each candidate for political discussion and debates. The amount of time devoted to advertising and promotions should be subject to reasonable limits and "infomercials" should be prohibited.

If propaganda is published in the form of purported studies or reports from "think tanks" there should be accompanying information about the bias of such sources, which usually describe themselves as nonpartisan research organizations.

The Internet must be kept free of control by government or private monopolies and available for discussion of alternative points of view. Independent media must be able to report on a global basis (www.indymedia.org). Low-power radio should be reasonably available for local organizations to provide information independent of the mainstream media. Unreasonable copyright and patent provisions need to be reversed.

Banking policies enlarge the income gap

Corporations, of course, act according to the wishes of those wealthy persons who vote the controlling stock. According to a World Bank study, the top one percent in the world's population (about 50 million of the five billion) had 9.5% of the world's income in 1993, while the whole bottom half had only 8.5%. According to a UN study, only

1.4% of the world's income in 1992 went to the 20% who live in the world's poorest countries.

Wealth is known to be quite concentrated at present, although recent global figures are hard to find, especially for wealth rather than income. Federal Reserve figures for 1989 showed that the richest 1% of American households accounted for nearly 40% of the nation's wealth, and the top 20% accounted for 80% of the wealth. The rich, of course, prefer not to disclose such information, so the gap may be understated.

With wealth goes power. Powerful banking families have long influenced public policy and financed wars. The interests of today's major financial houses and corporations are promoted by the International Monetary Fund (IMF) and the World Bank (both created at the Bretton Woods Conference in 1944 during World War II), and by other agencies for export financing and regional development.

The original purpose of the World Bank was to provide financial aid by making and insuring loans where needed to promote economic recovery throughout the world. That of the IMF was to maintain fixed and stable exchange rates among the currencies of member nations. When currencies were allowed to "float" in the 1970s, the IMF took on a new mission similar to the World Bank. It offered loans (with conditions) to developing countries and guaranteed loans with similar conditions by international private banks.

When a currency crisis occurs, the IMF remedy is to demand austerity and deregulation in exchange for additional loans or loan extensions. Typically, there is no demand for punishment of corrupt politicians, but there are demands to give foreign corporations more access to domestic markets, speed up the opening of branch offices by foreign banks and stock companies, privatize government operations, reduce social welfare programs, and relax protections of workers, consumers, and the environment.

Sometimes, when speculators bet against their currency, governments or their central banks try to prop up national currencies at the expense of the public—generally an expensive and futile effort. One proposal to discourage wild speculation is the "Tobin tax" of the late Nobel-Prize-winning Yale economist James Tobin, promoted by Attac, a 27,000-member organization in France. By agreement among nations, financial transactions would be subject to a small tax for international aid. Another proposal to stabilize exchange rates would be to base currencies on actual commodities rather than existing credit money created by banks.

Most, perhaps all, currency throughout the world is now redeemable only for more paper, and its purchasing power depends wholly on public confidence. Banks create money by simply crediting a customer's account with a balance equal to the amount of a loan document signed by the customer. Since the balances in customers' bank accounts are not all claimed at once, banks are able to issue such credits amounting to many times the bank's capital, the ratio being set by bank regulators.

Ostensibly to protect the public against inflation, and to safeguard banks' profits, central banks take deflationary measures whenever there is a hint of inflation, often resulting in a calamitous rise in unemployment. When financial firms "too big to fail" are in trouble, central banks call on the government to bail them out with public funds. This encourages risk taking by the banks with the consequences at public expense.

In the United States, the Federal Reserve Board (which issues the dollars that have become the *de facto* medium for international exchange) sets interest rates independently of any elected officials, as is also the case now with the Bank of England and the new European Central Bank. They all have the same "neo-liberal" economic philosophy as the FRB, the World Bank, and the IMF.

Their "scarce money" policies keep people unemployed because potential customers for the goods they would produce lack the money to buy them, and businesses will not hire workers if there is no market for the products. In an effort to develop markets businesses often try to turn faddish luxuries into necessities, which can lead to foolish waste of natural resources. To facilitate consumerism credit card debt (at exorbitant rates) has been promoted so irresponsibly it resembles a house of cards waiting to collapse—and banks in the U.S. have successfully lobbied Congress for a law that tends to close off any escape from credit card debt through personal bankruptcy filings.

Based on expedients used during the 1930s Depression when economic deadlock reached a peak, various arrangements for barter, community currency, and mutual credit have come into use.

One of the best known is Michael Linton's Local Employment Trading System (LETS), also known as Local Exchange Trading System. Computer software is available that makes it easy for a community to set up such a system (www.cyberclass.net). Other community currencies have been developed in Ithaca (New York), Argentina, Brazil, Uruguay, Chile, and Spain (www.cyberclass.net/argentina.htm). Long-term borrowing is also provided by WIR in Switzerland (www.wir.ch—in French, German, and Italian) and JAK in Sweden (www.jak.se—in English).

In addition to community currencies are proposals for commodity-backed currencies for the purpose of resolving inequities in foreign currency exchanges, including the Terra, expressed as a specified basket of raw materials, proposed by Bernard Lietaer, a former senior executive of the central bank of Belgium. Unless non-traditional systems can replace conventional banking and fiat money, there still remains the need to reform the national and international systems that dominate the world economy. Any international organizations such as IMF, the World Bank, and various regional development agencies that make grants or loans to assist nations in financial crises should not be under the exclusive control of bankers; they should be responsible and accountable to elected representatives of the world's people and should not be allowed to operate in secret.

The superiority of mind over matter

In dealing with the harmful effects of excessive materialism, people may turn to spiritual and philosophical insights. Most people recognize values that go beyond personal satisfaction. Although material progress has relieved the grinding burdens of many, its excesses can undermine quality of life. There are also large numbers of people still struggling for mere existence. To achieve global reforms there must be awakened in people the yearning to see purpose in life and to help make the world a better place.

Contrary to the assertions of some religious zealots, there are noble motives in many nonbelievers. One can find both good and bad in the devout as well as the nonbelievers. They can work together for good when they respect each other's freedom of thought. It is possible to draw on sources of inspiration from various cultures as well as inner resources.

Spirituality aids the progress of human beings, regarding them as more than physical bodies, having souls, selves, minds and/or personalities. It aims to harmonize the self with infinity, which implies a common bond among all human beings.

Society should make sure that everyone has access to the physical necessities of life and to opportunity for spiritual progress. A good example is the best teacher. Animals and plants, as well as people, should be treated with love and respect.

After thousands of years of the "dominator paradigm," exploiting the environment for whatever humans want, earth is in a crisis. Neglect and abuse of the earth's ecological systems threatens life on the planet while soaring population places increasing demands on earth's resources. Unwise agricultural practices have turned much fertile land into desert, and the loss of topsoil makes feeding a growing population more difficult.

Millions of individuals around the world have recognized this problem and nourished a movement for "sustainable living" based on a greater degree of local self-sufficiency based on cooperation rather than competition. Communities formed on this basis could conduct life-time learning and work together in regions to form a bottom-up system of international governance.

For any type of self-government literacy and education are important so that people can base their decisions on facts that they are able to understand. This is especially true when political corruption, media concentration, and subsidized propaganda machines are rampant. Unfortunately, these influences also infect education at all levels.

Compulsory free education, pioneered in the U.S. in the 19th century and taken as a model for universal education in other countries, not only prepared people from farms to work in factories but also provided a useful background for citizenship. Government support of higher education for U.S. veterans of World War II (The GI Bill) was also a documented success.

In recent years, studies have shown declines in academic performance in the U.S., along with a rise in youth crime and sexual promiscuity, which some people blame on the Supreme Court decision that banned mandatory public prayer in the public schools. A more likely explanation lies in unwise educational innovations, such as dubious psychological valuations on report cards, stress on peer approval, abandonment of phonetic aids to reading, questionable "new" math, neglect of geography and history, grade inflation and social promotion, and weakening of discipline in school and at home.

Today's rapidly changing world may call for another revolution in education, fostering natural curiosity and joy of learning rather than overemphasis on training for jobs. In the more developed nations very few people work on assembly lines any more. Neither there nor in the factory towns of less developed countries does the traditional pattern prevail of mothers staying home to raise children.

The world has become more complex, with each person becoming a node of a network within networks, constantly changing and enabled by electronic communication across huge distances. The old idea of schooling that prepared one for a lifetime job is obsolete. In advanced societies students must expect career changes that will require adaptation. In other places ways of life that were unchanged for generations may become impossible because of manmade or natural changes. This makes it vital that education develop versatility and adaptability, as well as providing for continuing intellectual growth.

People have an innate need for extended family or community, along with pondering the purpose of life—a place where personal material gain is sublimated to the common good. If this is not found in the family, it may lead one to the gang, secret society, or cult, and when the need for belonging is not met in a healthy way it may break out in violence. However, communities are now beginning to reach out in cooperation beyond the limits of family, tribe, nation, and religion. A promising development involves Community Learning and Information Centers (CLICs). (www.creatinglearningcommunities.org)

Learning Communities could replace government schools, adapting to change and providing opportunities for all their citizens through the milieu of libraries, museums, parks, farms, factories, businesses, homes, and the streets. Learning Communities are themselves learning and evolving, they are communities that provide learning, and they are communities of self-learners. They can be the foundation for the larger society.

Not all persons learn in the same way, so rote instruction is inefficient. Unless and until a new learning system emerges, there is need for serious reform in elementary and secondary education, as well as the universities.

Global reform is a do-it-yourself project

An overall conclusion of this study is that the future of Planet Earth and its people is too important to delegate to professional specialists. We cannot just leave peace negotiations to the diplomats, war to the generals and admirals, monetary policy to the bankers, natural resources to the miners and drillers, self-government to the politicians, and international commerce to secret trade negotiators. Nor can we leave unemployment and poverty problems to the economists of financial institutions, communication and information to the media oligarchy, food and drug safety to the manufacturers, our spiritual convictions to theologians, and learning to educational administrators.

People can make progress on two fronts. They can cooperate to work for more responsible behavior by governments, businesses, and organizations that run the world. And they can cooperatively organize their own lives to be less affected by the negative aspects of modern life. The need is more urgent than most people realize.

Modern communications technology can make the task easier. Throughout this book we have included links to sources of information and helpful organizations that readers can use according to their individual focus of interest. Many additional books and Internet links are presented in the next chapter. May you find many allies in the struggle for human betterment and solutions to the perils that threaten the earth.

10

Finding out the Truth

Given the bias and gaps in news coverage by the mass media, it is not easy to keep up with events in the struggle for global justice. To be informed we must turn to alternative media, including books that are not necessarily on the best-sellers list.

The following books and web sites have been recommended by one or more members of the FixGov forum as helpful in the context of our discussions. The editors are familiar with some of the works and sources cited, but certainly not all of them. There is no guarantee, of course, that the content is always consistent with the viewpoint of the FixGov forum participants. Readers will form their own judgements.

The lists are rather long and may seem too formidable. We encourage you to look through them rather quickly for sources that match your own areas of greatest interest.

BOOKS:

In case a book is incompletely identified below, you may wish to consult www.powells.com or www.amazon.com for further information, where you can obviously also order the book if you wish.

Ashford, Robert and Rodney Shakespeare [email address: Rodney.Shakespeare1@btopenworld.com], *Binary Economics-the new Paradigm* (Lanham, MD: University Press of America, 1999)

Bell, Jim, *Achieving Eco-nomic Security On Spaceship Earth* (on the Internet at http://www.jimbell.com/) ["a nuts and bolts, how to, common sense book about how to use free-market-forces to revitalize our national and world economies in ways that are completely ecologically sustainable."]

Black, Jan Knippers, *Inequity in the Global Village, Recycled Rhetoric and Disposable People* (Kumerian Press)

Blum, William, *Rogue State—a Guide to the World's Only Superpower* (Monroe, Maine: Common Courage Press, 2000)

Bossel, Hartmut, *Earth at a Crossroads, Paths to a Sustainable Future*, (Cambridge: Cambridge University Press, 1998)

Boulding, Kenneth, *The Economics of the Coming Spaceship Earth* (1971)

Bridges, William, *Job Shift, How to Prosper in A Workplace Without Jobs* (Addison-Wesley Publishing Company)

Bridges, William, *Managing Transitions, Making the Most of Change*

Broder, David S., *Democracy Derailed: Initiative Campaigns and The Power of Money* (A James H. Silberman Book, Harcourt, Inc., 2000)

Brower, Michael, and Warren Leon, *The Consumer's Guide to Effective Environmental Choices: Practical Advice from the Union of Concerned Scientists* (Union of Concerned Scientists, 1999)

Brubaker, Sterling, *To Live on Earth: Man and His Environment in Perspective* (The John Hopkins Press, 1972)

Burdick, Eugene, and William J. Lederer, *The Ugly American* [A classic book about how the U.S. approached Vietnam in the 1950s, but could just as well refer to American involvement in the Arab world today. The title has a double meaning: The physically ugly

American had the kindest heart; the powerful and ignorant American officials were "ugly" in their behavior.]

Bunzl, John, *The Simultaneous Policy: An Insider's Guide to Saving Humanity and the Planet* (London: New European Publications, 2001) [The basis of a global movement for cooperation among nations to bring multinational corporations and finance under control. The author is also the founder of the International Simultaneous Policy Organisation, operating in some 20 countries.]

Caldicott, Helen, *If You Love This Planet: A Plan to Heal the Earth*

Caldwell, Lyton Keith, *Environment: A Challenge to Modern Society* (Garden City, NY: Anchor Books, Double Day & Company, 1971)

Cavanagh, John [see International Forum on Globalization]

Ceballos-Lascurain, Hector, *Tourism, Ecotourism and Protected Areas* (IV World Congress on National Parks and Protected Areas-IUCN Protected Areas Programme)

Center for Economic and Policy Research, *Growth May Be Good for the Poor-But are IMF and World Bank Policies Good for Growth?*

Center for Public Integrity, *Citizen Muckraking: How to Investigate and Right Wrongs in Your Community* (Common Courage Press)

Chossudovsky, Michel, *The Globalization Of Poverty—Impacts of IMF and World Bank Reforms* (Penang, Malaysia: The Third World Network, 1997)

Covey, Stephen, *The Seven Habits of Highly Effective People-Powerful Lessons in Personal Change* (Simon & Schuster)

Covey, Stephen, *Principle-Centered Leadership* (Simon & Schuster)

Cummins, Ronnie and Ben Lilliston, *Genetically Engineered Foods: A Self-Defense Guide for Consumers* (Marlowe & Company)

Daily, Gretchen C. and Paul R. Ehrlich, *Population, Sustainability, and Earth's Carrying Capacity: A framework for estimating population sizes and lifestyles that could be sustained without undermining future generations* (BioScience, 1992)

DeVilliers, Marq, *Water-The Fate of Our Most Precious Resource*

Diamond, Jared, *Guns, Germs, and Steel*, (London: W.W. Norton, 1997)

Douthwaite, Richard, *The Growth Illusion* (Lilliput Press, Dublin, 1992)

Drucker, Peter F., *Managing for The Future*

Eisler, Riene, *The Chalice and the Blade* [re the "Dominator Paradigm"]

Elgin, Duane, and Coleen LeDrew, *Global Paradigm Report: Tracking the Shift Underway*

Eyerman, Ron, and Andrew Jamison, *Social Movements: A Cognitive Approach* (University Park: Pennsylvania State University Press, 1991)

Peter Farb, Peter, *Man's Rise to Civilization* (New York: EP Dutton, 1968)

Foreign Affairs, a journal published quarterly by the Council on Foreign Relations, New York

Fresia, Jerry, *Toward an American Revolution-Exposing the Constitution and Other Illusions* (Boston: South End Press, 1988)

Fuller, Buckminster, *Critical Path*

Gelspan, Ross, *The Heat Is On: The Climate Crisis, The Cover-Up, The Prescription* (Perseus Books, 1998)

Gore, Albert, *Earth in the Balance* (1992) [Written by the former U.S. vice president and 2000 presidential candidate.]

Greco, Thomas H., *Money: Understanding and Creating Alternatives to Legal Tender*, (Chelsea Green, 2002) [A major critique of fiat money controlled by private bankers.]

Greider, William, *Who Will Tell the People, the Betrayal of American Democracy* (New York: Touchstone-Simon & Schuster, 1993)

Greider, William, *One World Ready or Not, the Manic Logic of Global Capitalism*, (New York: Simon & Schuster, 1997)

Goldsmith, James, *The Response* (London: Macmillan, 1995)

Hawken, Paul, *The Ecology of Commerce, A Declaration of Sustainability*

Hawken, Paul, Amory Lovins and L. Hunter Lovins, *Natural Capitalism: Creating the Next Industrial Revolution* (Little, Brown & Company)

Heilbronner, Robert, *Twenty-first Century Capitalism* (1992)

Henderson, Hazel, *Beyond Globalization: Shaping a Sustainable Global Economy*

Henderson, Hazel, *Building a Win-Win World* (Kumarian Press)

Hertz, Noreena, *The Silent Takeover*

Honey, Martha, *Ecotourism & Sustainable Development-Who Owns Paradise?* (Island Press)

Huntington, Samuel P., *The Clash of Civilizations and the Remaking of World Order* (London: Simon and Schuster, 1997)

International Forum on Globalization, *Alternatives to Economic Globalization: A Better World Is Possible* (San Francisco: Berrett-Koehler, 2002)

Isaak, Robert, Green Logic, *Ecopreneurship, Theory & Ethics* (Kumerian Press)

Judis, John B., *The Paradox of American Democracy, Elites, Special Interests, and the Betrayal of Public Trust*

Kelso, Louis O. and Mortimer J. Adler, *The Capitalist Manifesto* (New York: Random House, 1958)

Kelso, Louis O. and Mortimer J. Adler, *The New Capitalists: A Proposal for Freeing Growth from the Slavery of Savings* (New York: Random House, 1961) [Kelso and Adler books, and other Kelso writings, are accessible free from the web site of the Kelso Institute for the Study of Economic Systems at www.kelsoinstitute.org/]

Kohr, Leopold, *The Breakdown of Nations* (London: New European Publications, 2001)

Korten, David C., *The Post Corporate World—Life after Capitalism* (West Hartford, Connecticut: Kumerian Press, 1999)

Korten, David C., *When Corporations Rule the World* (West Hartford, Connecticut: Kumerian Press, 1995) [Detailed examples of third world disasters and admitted failures of the World Bank and IMF.]

Lappé, Frances Moore, Joseph Collins, and Peter Rosset, *World Hunger, Twelve Myths* (Grove Press, New York, 1986)

Lietaer, Bernard, *The Future of Money: a new way to create wealth, work and a wiser world* (Century/Random House, 2001) [Former high official of the central bank in Belgium.]

Logan, Ron, PROUT: *A New Approach to Socio-Economic Development*

Lundberg, Ferdinand, *The Rich and the Super Rich: A Study in the Power of Money Today,* (New York: Lyle Stuart, 1968)

Mander, Jerry, and Edward Goldsmith (eds.), *The Case Against the Global Economy and for a Turn Toward The Local* (San Francisco: Sierra Club Books, 1996)

Manning, Richard, *Grasslands* (concerning agricultural problems)

Martin, Hans-Peter, and Harald Schumann, *The Global Trap: Globalization and the Assault on Democracy and Prosperity* (St. Martin's Press, New York, 1997)

McChesney, Robert, *Rich Media, Poor Democracy* (University of Illinois Press,1999) [further information can be found at www.robertmcchesney.com].

McCloskey, David, *Ecology and Community: The Bioregional Vision*

McLaren, Deborah, *Rethinking Tourism and Ecotravel, The Paving of Paradise and What You Can Do To Stop It* (Kumerian Press)

Moore, Richard K., *Escaping the Matrix*

Muir, Diana, *Reflections in Bullough's Pond: Economy and Ecosystem*

Ohmae, Kenichi, *End of The Nation State-The Rise of Regional Economies, How new engines of prosperity are reshaping global markets*

O'Shah, Nasrucin, The Zen of Global Transformation, (Wexford Ireland: Quay Largo Productions, 2002) (http://www.quaylargo.com/Transformaticn/)

Parenti, Michael, *The Sword and the Dollar, Imperialism, Revolution, and the Arms Race* (New York: St. Martin's Press, 1989)

Parenti, Michael, *History as Mystery* (San Francisco, City Lights Books, 1999)

Parenti, Michael, *Make-Believe Media-The Politics of Entertainment* (New York: St. Martin's Press, 1992)

Parenti, Michael, *Inventing Reality-The Politics of News Media* (New York: St. Martin's Press, 1993)

Peters, Tom, *Thriving on Chaos-Handbook for a Management Revolution*

Phillips, Kevin, *Arrogant Capital* (Boston: Little, Brown and Company, 1994) [Major changes in the U.S. political system to restore citizen control of government proposed by a Republican political analyst of Nixon's 1988 campaign who has since criticized Reagan's tax cuts for the rich and corporations.]

Quinn, Daniel, *The Story of B* (London: Bantam Books, 1996)

Rawls, John, *Law of Peoples* (1999)

Rawls, John, *Political Liberalism* (1993)

Rawls, John, *A Theory of Justice* (1971)

Ray and Anderson, *The Cultural Creatives*

Rifkin, Jeremy, *Beyond Beef*

Rifkin, Jeremy, *The End of Work-Technology, Jobs and Your Future*

Rifkin, Jeremy, *The Decline of the Global Labor Force and the Dawn of the Post-Market Era* (G. P. Putnam & Sons)

Rifkin, Jeremy, *Beyond Beef, The Rise & Fall of the Cattle Culture* (Penguin Books)

Robbins, John, *Diet for A New America, How Your Food Choices Affect Your Health, Happiness and Future of Life On Earth* (Stillpoint Publishing)

Robbins, John, *Diet for A New World*

Robbins, John, *Food Revolution*

Rough, Jim, *Society's Breakthrough!: Releasing Essential Wisdom and Virtue in All the People,* (Bloomington, Indiana: 1stPublishing, 2002)

Ruckelshaus, William, "Toward a Sustainable World" (Scientific American, Sept. 1989)

Sandoz, Maria, *Crazy Horse: Strange Man of the Oglalas* (50th Anniversary Edition, University of Nebraska Press, 1992)

Schipper, Lee, Ruth Steiner, and Stephen Meyers, "Trends in Transportation Energy Use, 1970-1988: An International Perspective", in *Transportation And Global Climate Change*, edited by David L. Green and Danilo J. Santini, published by the American Council for an Energy-Efficient Economy, Washington, D.C., and Berkeley, California, 1993

Schumacher, E. F., *Small is Beautiful* (1973).

Shapiro, Howard-Yana, and John Harrisson, *Gardening for the Future of the Earth*

Sklar, Holly (ed.), *Trilateralism-the Trilateral Commission and Elite Planning for World Management* (South End Press, Boston, 1980)

Simon, D. and A. Naaman (eds.) *Development as Theory and Practice* (Harlow: Addison Wesley Longman & DARG, RGS-IBG, 2000)

Simon, Joel, *Endangered Mexico: An Environment on The Edge* (Sierra Club Books)

Simone, Charles B., *Cancer and Nutrition*

Sitarz, Daniel, *AGENDA 21-The Earth Summit Strategy to Save Our Planet*

Sobel, Robert, *The Great Boom, How a Generation of Americans Created the World's Most Prosperous Society*

Soros, George, *Open Society, Reforming Global Capitalism* [By the currency speculator who made a fortune on the collapse of the British pound sterling but has since advocated global reform.]

Steen, Athena, Bill Steen, David Bainbridge, and David Eisenberg *The Straw Bale Housebook* (A Real Goods Independent Living Book)

Stimson, Richard A., *Playing with the numbers. How So-called Experts Mislead Us about the Economy* (Westchester Press, 1999) [Facts are presented to expose the misinformation spread by official sources about the U.S. and world economy; for excerpts from book, reviews, etc.: www.stimson.homestead.com]

Thoren, Theodore R., and Richard Warner, *The Truth in Money Book* (ISBN:0960693874; 4th rev edition, April 1994) [It gives a scientific analysis of the federal reserve monetary system, including how banks legally create money and how the system is designed so there is more debt than money to pay it back—James McGuigan].

Toffler, Alvin, *The Third Wave* (1980) [Futurist author whose best sellers also include *Future Shock*.]

Vanderbilt, Tom, *The Sneaker Book-Anatomy of An Industry, Bottom Line Marketing & Advertising* (The New Press)

Vidal, Gore, *Perpetual War for Perpetual Peace: How We Got To Be So Hated* (2002)

Wallach, Lori and Michelle Sforza, *Whose Trade Organization?* (Public Citizen)

Wasserman, Harvey, *The Last Energy War: The Battle over Utility Deregulation* (Seven Stories Press)

Weisman, Alan, *Gaviotas, A Village to Reinvent the World* (Chelsea Green Publishing Company)

Wolman, William, and Anne Colamosca, *The Judas Economy: The Triumph of Capital and the Betrayal of Work* (Addison-Wesley, 1997)

Zinn, Howard, *A People's History of the United States* (New York: Harper Collins, 1989)

WEB SITES:

The following web addresses have each been recommended by at least one member of the FixGov forum. Explanatory descriptions have been included in most cases, often as supplied by the sites themselves, which are therefore responsible for the accuracy of the description. The authors and editors do not necessarily agree with statements and opinions on these sites. For convenience the listings have been arranged in categories generally following the chapters, although some overlapping occurs. For example, some sites that could be listed as Global and National Action appear instead under the topics to which they relate.

The editors regret if any sites may turn out not to be accessible by the time you try them.

Globalization Problems

Agenda 21 & Other UNCED Agreements
http://www.igc.org/habitat/agenda21/

Bilderberg
http://www.bilderberg.org/
        The High Priests of Globalization

Buckminster Fuller Institute
http://www.bfi.org/
        Economic and political analysis by the genius inventor of the geodesic dome.

Bretton Woods Project
http://www.brettonwoodsproject.org/
        Critical Voices on the IMF and World Bank.

CIA. Global Trends 2015
http://www.odci.gov/cia/publications/globaltrends2015/index.html
        A Dialogue about the Future with Nongovernmental Experts.

Covert Action
http://www.covertaction.org/
        Keeps you up-to-date on covert activities, cover-ups, military affairs, and current trouble spots. Contributors include many ex-intelligence officers who saw the error of their ways.

Earth Charter
http://www.earthcharter.org/
        "We must join together to bring forth a sustainable global society founded on respect for nature, universal human rights, economic justice, and a culture of peace. Towards this end, it is imperative

that we, the peoples of Earth, declare our responsibility to one another, to the greater community of life, and to future generations."

Global Exchange
http://www.globalexchange.org/
"Global Exchange is a human rights organization dedicated to promoting environmental, political, and social justice around the world. Since our founding in 1988, we have been striving to increase global awareness among the US public while building international partnerships around the world."
http://www.globalexchange.org/economy/
http://www.globalexchange.org/wbimf/links.html
World Bank/IMF Links.

Global Issues that affect everyone
http://www.globalissues.org/
Maintained by Anup Shah in his spare time and at his own expense. All information presented is well documented with links to sources.

Global Village or Global Pillage?
http://www.villageorpillage.org/

Growth May Be Good for the Poor—But are IMF and World Bank Policies Good for Growth?
http://www.cepr.net/response_to_dollar_kraay.htm
A Closer Look at the World Bank's Most Recent Defense of Its Policies.

International Forum on Gloalization (IFG)
http://www.ifg.org/
The IFG first met in 1994 in the wake of NAFTA and the Uruguay Round of GATT, recognizing that global governance was being taken over by transnational corporations and their international trade bureaucracies. Begun as a think tank among some thirty people

(later expanded to over sixty), the IFG favors new international agreements that place the needs of people, local economies, and the natural world ahead of the interest of corporations.

Multinational Monitor's on-line database
http://www.essential.org/monitor/monitor.html
    World Bank, IMF, environmental and labor issues, searchable back issues, and links to other sources on corporate and international issues.

Open Democracy
http://www.opendemocracy.net
    Forum on Globalisation.

Poverty in Africa—World Bank
http://www4.worldbank.org/afr/poverty/default.htm

Secession Network
http://secession.net/
    "At least 5,000 ethnic, linguistic and racial groups are lumped together into only 189 nation states. Most of the world's violent conflicts are related to struggles for dominance within or independence from some large, multi-national nation state. A large portion of the world's people would choose to secede from their respective nation states if given the opportunity."

United Nations-Universal Declaration of Human Rights
http://www.un.org/rights/50/decla.htm

World Watch Institute
http://www.worldwatch.org/

Environmental Issues

Audubon Society Online
http://www.audubon.org/

Bullfrog Films
http://www.bullfrogfilms.com/
        Environmental and Educational Videos.

Capitol Report-Environmental News Links
http://www.caprep.com/

Centre for Science and Environment
http://www.cseindia.org/index.html

Climate Neutral Travelling
http://www.triplee.com/

Climate Solutions-Publications
http://climatesolutions.org/global_warming_is_here/index.html

Columbia University Studies
http://www.ciesin.columbia.edu/indicators/ESI/ESI_01a.pdf
        2001 Environmental Sustainability Index.
http://www.ciesin.columbia.edu/indicators/ESI/ESI_01b.pdf
        Country Profiles.

Earth Emergency
www.earthemergency.org
        "A Call to Action is bringing together non governmental organisations and activists and local and global networks around an agreed agenda, based on a planetary ethic of respect for all life and human dignity and to urge governments worldwide to join us in using the coming decade to adopt the new thinking and actions required to restore the earth and secure a sustainable future for present and coming generations."

Earth First Journal
http://www.earthfirstjournal.org/
        Radical Environmental Journal

Earth from Space-Earth Observatory
http://earth.jsc.nasa.gov/

Earth Science Image Gallery
http://www.earth.nasa.gov/gallery/index.html

Eco-Standards for Multinationals
http://ens.lycos.com/ens/sep2000/2000L-09-01-01.html
Multinationals with High Eco-Standards Most Likely to Succeed.

Environment.org (UK)
http://www.environment.org.uk/activist/

Federation of American Scientists
http://www.fas.org/

Friends of the Earth
http://www.foe.org
Opposes genetically engineered food, and has sued to force cost-benefit analysis of the US Forest Service's logging program.

Genetically Engineered Food
http://www.greenpeaceusa.org/ge
"Green Peace website fighting genetically engineered food in Kellogg's cereal and other products. Kellogg promises not to use genetically modified organisms (GMOs) in their cereal sold in Europe, but refuses that promise to Americans."

Green Innovations (Australia)
http://www.green-innovations.asn.au/

Institute for Agriculture and Trade Policy
http://www.iatp.org/
IATP promotes resilient family farms, rural communities and ecosys-

tems around the world through research and education, science and technology, and advocacy.

Lindzen on ClimateChange
http://www.cato.org/pubs/regulation/reg15n2g.html
Global Warming: The Origin and Nature of the Alleged Scientific Consensus, Richard S. Lindzen, the Alfred P. Sloan Professor of Meteorology at the Massachusetts Institute of Technology. (Opponent of the global warming theories.)

Oil Resources
http://www.hubbertpeak.com/index.asp
Named after the late Dr. M. King Hubbert, geophysicist, this website provides data, analysis and recommendations regarding the upcoming peak in the rate of global oil extraction.

Planet Drum
http://www.planetdrum.org/
"Developed the concept of a bioregion: a distinct area with coherent and interconnected plant and animal communities, and natural systems, often defined by a watershed."

Public Interest Research Groups
http://www.pirg.org/enviro/superfund
Grassroot campaign to make polluters, not taxpayers, pay for clean up of toxic waste sites

Rainforest Action Network
http://www.ran.org/

Resource Center on Business, the Environment and the Bottom Line
http://www.greenbiz.com/

Sierra Club (USA)
http://www.sierraclub.org/

"Protecting the Environment…For Our Families, For Our Future."

United Nations System-wide Earth Watch
http://www.earthwatch.unep.net
Earthwatch is a United Nations initiative to coordinate and share UN-wide information on the global environment

World Scientists' Warning To Humanity
http://www.deoxy.org/sciwarn.htm

Economic and Financial Topics

Achieving Eco-nomic Security on Spaceship Earth
http://www.jimbell.com
A nuts and bolts, how to, common sense book about how to use free-market-forces to revitalize our national and world economies in ways that are completely ecologically sustainable. Jim Bell is an independent broadcaster in California. His radio show at 10-11 p.m. Sundays can be heard on the Internet.

Campaign for America's Future
http://www.ourfuture.org
For a budget that meets social needs rather than favoring the rich and the war machine

Chossudovsky on Global Finance and Poverty
http://www.transnational.org/features/g7solution.html
The G7 "Solution" to the Global Financial Crisis-A Marshall Plan for Creditors and Speculators by Michel Chossudovsky.
http://www.transnational.org/features/chossu_worldbank.html
Global Falsehoods: How the World Bank and the UNDP Distort the Figures on Global Poverty. By Michel Chossudovsky.

Economic Policy Institute
http://www.epinet.org
>   Provides information and links to various organizations.

Economic Policy News
http://www.epn.org/ideacentral/economic.html
>   Home page provides links to numerous non-governmental
organizations (NGOs).

Galbraith on Economic Fallacies
http://www.prospect.org/archives/V11-7/galbraith-j.html
>   "How the Economists Got It Wrong."

New Economics Foundation
http://www.neweconomics.org/

Progressive Utilization Theory (PROUT)
http://www.prout.org/index.html
>   "Economics for Human Development."

Redefining Progress
http://www.rprogress.org/index.html
>   Favors the "Genuine Progress Indicator" over misleading
GDP figures.

The True Majority
http://www.truemajority.org
>   Against squandering wealth on war

Political Systems

The Ballot Box
http://www.ballot-box.org/
>   "The Deception of a Democracy."

Black Radical Congress
http://www.blackradicalcongress.org/
  "Forging a Black Liberation Agenda for the 21ˢᵗ Century."

Capitol Strategy
http://www.capitolstrategy.com/
  Washington's Political Portal.

Center for Public Integrity
integrityhttp://www.publicintegrity.org/
    "to provide the American public with the findings of its investigations and analyses of public service, government accountability, and ethics-related issues via books, reports and newsletters."

CounterCoup
http://www.geocities.com/countercoup/
  No vote count, No victory! No justice. No peace!

Gore Won Site
http://www.geocities.com/dearkandb/

League of Women Voters (USA)
http://www.lwv.org/
    LWV, "a nonpartisan political organization, encourages the informed and active participation of citizens in government, works to increase understanding of major public policy issues, and influences public policy through education and advocacy."

Public Campaign
http://www.publiccampaign.org
    Working against campaign finance abuse

Nazis and the Republican Party
http://www.bartcop.com/nazigop.htm

Thomas Paine
http://tompaine.com/
        Inspired by the radical writer of the American Revolution, Thomas Paine.

Corporate Power

Corporation history
http://www.corporatewatch.org/pages/dan_corp.html
        "The creation & development of English commercial corporations and the abolition of democratic control over their behaviour."

Corporate Watch
http://www.corporatewatch.org/

Multinational Monitor
http://www.essential.org/monitor/
        Founded by Ralph Nader. September 2001 issue features "Bearing the Burden of IMF and World Bank Policies."

POCLAD
http://www.poclad.org/
        Programs on Corporations, Law and Democracy.

Top 100 Corporate Criminals of the Decade
http://www.corporatepredators.org/top100.html

World Economic Forum
http://www.weforum.org/
        Incorporated since 1971 as a foundation, it has become an institution comprised of the 1,000 most powerful corporations in the world. In 2002 it moved its annual meeting from from its traditional setting in Davos, Switzerland to New York in an act of solidarity with the city.

Monetary Systems

Cyberclass Network
http://www.cyberclass.net/
        Emphasis on community currencies vs. fiat money.

Cyberclass—LETS
http://www.cyberclass.net/bartable.htm
        LETS. Local Employment Trading System. Usury-free Community Currency.
http://www.cyberclass.net/turmel/urlsnat.htm
        700 LETS timetrading systems in 45 different countries.

Commodity Currencies
http://www.geog.le.ac.uk/ijccr/5no1.htm
        "Commodity Currencies for Fair and Stable International Exchange Rates.' By Walter Plinge.

Community Exchange Systems in Asia, Africa and Latin America
http://ccdev.lets.net/index2.html

Davies on Monetary History
http://www.ex.ac.uk/~RDavies/arian/llyfr.html
        History of Money from Ancient Times to the Present Day by Glyn Davies

Debt Slavery
http://www.cfoss.com/grip.html
        The Grip of Death: a study of modern money, debt slavery and destructive economics by Michael Rowbotham

Future of Money
http://www.cato.org/pubs/books/money/tableof.htm
        The future of money in the information age. Ed. by James A. Dorn

Greco on Community Currencies
http://www.ic.org/market/money/index.html
    New Money for Healthy Communities by Thomas H. Greco, Jr.

International Journal of Community Currency Research
http://www.geog.le.ac.uk/ijccr/
    "The aim of this journal is to provide a forum for the dissemination of knowledge and understanding about the emerging array of community currencies being used throughout the world both at present and in the past."

Islamic Banking
http://www.usc.edu/dept/MSA/economics/islamic_banking.html
    Islamic banking. By Mohamed Ariff, University of Malaya.
http://www.usc.edu/dept/MSA/economics/nbank1.html
    Principles of Islamic Banking.

Lietaer on Community Currencies
http://www.ratical.org/many_worlds/cc/CC.html
    Community Currencies. By Bernard Lietaer.

Menger on the origins of money
http://www.ecn.bris.ac.uk/het/menger/money.txt
    The origins of money. Carl Menger.

Mondragon Coop
http://www.mondragon.mcc.es/ingles/menu_ing.html
    Successful Cooperative in Spain.

Monetary Reform
http://www.electronz.cjb.net/
    Electronz. The New Zealand monetary reform weekly e-zine (edited by Don Bethune, QSM)

No Usury Net
http://www.nousury.net/
        Ed. by T.J. Kennedy.

Reinventing Money
http://www.communitycurrency.org/reweaveWeb.html
        Reinventing Money, Restoring the Earth, Reweaving the Web
of Life. By Carol Brouillet.

Shann Turnbull of Australia on money and banking http://
members.optusnet.com.au/~sturnbull>

Communications Media

Cronkite on the Media
http://www.mediachannel.org/originals/cronkite.shtml
        Famous American TV newsman Walter Cronkite's comments
on the media.

FAIR
www.fair.org
        An organization dedicated to "Fairness & Accuracy in Report-
ing" (FAIR), that has email notices and a website to expose incomplete
and/or inaccurate information in the media.

McChesney on the Media
http://www.robertmcchesney.com
        Criticism of the media by a communications professor at the
University of Illinois at Urbana-Champaign.

Media Watchers and Activists
http://www.uiowa.edu/~commstud/resources/media/
mediawatch.html
        Civil organisations that participate in Media Watch: a model
for civic action.

PR Watch
http://www.prwatch.org/
     Exposing the activities of secretive, little-known propaganda-for-hire firms that work to control political debates and public opinion.

UN World Summit on the Information Society.
http://www.itu.int/wsis/
     What values do we embrace to ensure that the Information Society becomes a vehicle for democracy, justice, equality, the respect for individuals and peoples, their personal and social development?

Alternative News

American Partisan (Internet magazine)
http://www.americanpartisan.com/
     "Hard Hitting Commentary and Informative News."

American Prospect, The (USA)
http://www.prospect.org/
     A Magazine of Politics, Policy and Culture.

Arianna on Line
http://www.ariannaonline.com/
     Arianna Huffington is a nationally syndicated columnist and author of eight books. She conducted a "shadow convention" to expose hypocrisy in U.S. major party conventions. In her book, *How To Overthrow the Government*, she "describes how America has been torn in two—divided between a moneyed elite getting rich from globalization and an increasing number of citizens left choking on the dust of Wall Street's galloping bulls."

Blue Ear Forum
http://www.blueear.com/
     "Global Writing Worth Reading." Journalists and authors

from many countries write on observations, comment, books, travel, etc.

Deep Dish TV
http://www.deepdishtv.org
    "A national satellite network, linking local access producers and programmers, independent video makers, activists, and other individuals who support the idea and reality of a progressive television network."

Environmental Media Services
http://www.ems.org/

Environment News Service
http://ens.lycos.com/aboutens.html

Harry Timez Link Page
http://www.sboa.se/harry/harryharry.html
    Maintained by a Swedish journalist, in English. Brief excerpts and links to current news and comment in major publications.

Indymedia-independent media reports
http://www.indymedia.org
    Eyewitness reports from protest meetings against WTO, IMF and World Bank abuses, such as at Seattle, at the Republican and Democratic conventions, and at Quebec, Genoa, Washington, etc.

Mother Jones Magazine— The MoJo Wire
http://www.motherjones.com/
    "Daily News and Resources for the Sceptical Citizen."

Paper Tiger Television (PTTV)
http://www.papertiger.org
    "An open, non-profit, volunteer video collective. Through the production and distribution of our public access series, media literacy/video production workshops, community screenings and grass-

roots advocacy PTTV works to challenge and expose the corporate control of mainstream media."

Project Censored at Sonoma State University in California
http://www.projectcensored.org
Weekly release of important news under-covered by mainstream press.
http://www.sonoma.edu/projectcensored/
Annual lists of the most neglected and the most over-covered news stories in the mainstream media.

Prospect Magazine (UK)
http://www.prospect-magazine.co.uk/
"*Prospect* is the magazine for the intellectually curious general reader who appreciates finely written essays across the spectrum of political, intellectual and cultural debate. It is the intelligent monthly based in Britain—but with an international mind and an international readership."

World Daily Net
http://www.worldnetdaily.com/
"A Free Press For A Free People."

Znet and Zmag
http://www.zmag.org/
"A Community of People Concerned about Social Change." This is a major electronic magazine featuring many comments and interviews including ones with Noam Chomsky.

Alternative Life Styles

Alternet on Cultural Creatives
http://www.alternet.org/creatives.html
50 Million Creatives?

Alternatives for Simple Living
http://www.simpleliving.org/

Bicycling Community Page
http://danenet.wicip.org/bcp/

Canelo Project Mexico
http://www.caneloproject.com/
  Straw bale and cob construction.

Co-Intelligence Institute
http://www.co-intelligence.org/
  "Co-intelligence is living well WITH each other and life, creatively using diversity and uniqueness, consciously evolving together in partnership with nature, transforming culture. Use it for organizational development, better family relations, community renewal, and creating a more just, democratic and sustainable society."

Development Center for Appropriate Technology
http://www.cyberbites.com/dcat/
  "DCAT fosters creative solutions for meeting current basic human needs in ways that preserve positive options for future generations."

Information Centre for Low-tech Sustainability
http://www.bagelhole.org/

Korten on Civil Society
http://cyberjournal.org/cj/authors/korten/CivilizingSociety.shtml
  David Korten on Civil Society. An Unfolding Cultural Struggle.

Straw Bale Building Technology
http://strawbale.archinet.com.au/

Sustainable Development UK
http://www.sustainable-development.gov.uk/

Sustainable Economics
http://www.sus-tec.freeserve.co.uk/
        The bimonthly newsletter of the Green Economy Working Group of the Green Party of England and Wales.

Turtle Island Earth Stewards
http://www.ties.bc.ca/

Education

Coalition for Self-Learning (CLC)
http://www.creatinglearningcommunities.org/

Northwest Earth Institute
http://www.nwei.org/
        "NWEI is a pioneer in taking earth-centered education programs to people where they spend their time—in their neighborhoods, workplaces, homes, schools, and centers of faith."

Plug into the Sun (UK)
http://www.pluggingintothesun.org.uk/
        Educational Resources and Workshops in Energy Efficiency, Renewable Energy and Sustainable Development

Transforming Human Culture
http://www.earley.org/Transformation/
transforming_human_culture.htm
        Transforming Human Culture: Social Evolution and the Planetary Crisis by Jay Earley

Turtle Island Institute
http://www.tii-kokopellispirit.org

Kokopelli Spirit Ezine, Resource Guides, Communities, and Social Transformation (under construction)

Global and National Action

Aligning With Purpose…for a Better World
http://www.aligningwithpurpose.com/
    Jay Fenello's site: "Committed to peaceful, evolutionary change for the better. Here you will find assorted discussions and theories about what's wrong with our world, and what we can do about it. You will also find links to other sites consistent with our world view."

Alliance for Global Justice-50 Years is Enough Network
http://www.50years.org
    Opposing policies of World Bank and IMF.

Common Cause
http://www.commoncause.org
    Founded by Ralph Nader, "a non partisan citizen's group working for openness, honesty and accountability in government."

Congress Watchdog
http://www.congresswatchdog.org
    Public Citizen's site for voting records.

Focus on the global South
http://www.focusweb.org/

Foundation for Enterprise Development
http://www.fed.org/
    A non-profit organization dedicated to helping entrepreneurs and executives use employee ownership and equity compensation as a fair and effective means of motivating the workforce and improving corporate performance.

Mobilization for Global Justice
http://www.a16.org
        A key organization for the protest marches and demonstra-
tions against policies of the World Bank and IMF. Site includes reports
of past demonstrations.

Moore on Changing the World
http://cyberjournal.org/cj/guide/
        How the world works and how we can change it by Richard
Moore

People-Centered Development Forum (PCDForum)
http://iisd1.iisd.ca/pcdf/
        Founded by David Korten, "an international alliance of indi-
viduals and organizations dedicated to the creation of just, inclusive,
and sustainable human societies through voluntary citizen action."

Physicians for Social Responsibility (US affiliate of International Physicians for the Prevention of Nuclear War)
http://www.psr.org
        PSR opposes hazardous transport and use of plutonium for
nuclear energy plants around the world.

Protest.net
http://www.protest.net/
        A Calendar of Protest, Meetings and Conferences.

Public Citizen
http://www.citizen.org/
        Founded by Ralph Nader to reform American politics.

Simultaneous Policy
http://www.simpol.org/
        The International Simultaneous Policy Organisation (ISPO),
building support for commitments by all nations to restrain destructive

competition and promote global justice. Information on the book, *The Simultaneous Policy: An Insider's Guide to Saving Humanity and the Planet,* by John Bunzl.

Transnational Resource & Action Center
http://www.corpwatch.org/trac/about/trac.html
        "Counters corporate-led globalization through education and activism."

Union of Concerned Scientists
http://www.ucsusa.org/ucs-home.html

United Nations Reform
http://www.cunr.org
        Campaign for U.N. Reform offers a questionnaire to pin down your candidates on foreign policy questions

United Nations— Sustainable Development— Agenda 21
http://www.un.org/esa/sustdev/agenda21.htm

Vote Smart
http://www.vote-smart.org
        Project Vote Smart provides factual information on candidates' positions, voting records, backgrounds, and campaign financing.

World Federalist Association
http://www.wfa.org
        WFA works for more effective world government.

World Future Council
www.worldfuturecouncil.org
        "There is widespread global agreement on key values and action priorities. A council of respected individuals will be drawn from the wise, the heroes, the pioneers and the young. The moral power of this voice of global stewardship should not be underestimated. The core Council will meet periodically to hold hearings, commission

research and call for specific actions— which can be endorsed by the eParliament and brought into national parliaments by MPs for immediate legislative action, backed by the moral power of the WFC."

World Social Forum
http://www.forumsocialmundial.org.br/
          Forum Social Mundial.

About the Editors

Adriaan Boiten studied history and graduated from the Municipal University of Amsterdam in 1986. He served for 12 years in various municipal positions for historical preservation of the city. As the proprietor of a web design business he lives and works in the old inner city of Amsterdam.

Richard Stimson is an author and retired business professor in High Point, North Carolina. Educated at Yale, Florida International University, and the University of North Carolina at Chapel Hill, his careers have spanned association management, public relations, university teaching, and computer operations.

0-595-28067-6